THE ART *of*
BEING YOU

THE ART of BEING YOU

HOW TO LIVE AS
GOD'S MASTERPIECE

BOB KILPATRICK
JOEL KILPATRICK

ZONDERVAN

The Art of Being You
Copyright © 2010 by Bob Kilpatrick and Joel Kilpatrick

Requests for information should be addressed to:

Zondervan, 3900 *Sparks Dr. SE, Grand Rapids, Michigan 49546*

ISBN 978-0-310-34823-8 (softcover)

ISBN 978-0-310-32566-6 (audio edition)

ISBN 978-0-310-32567-3 (ebook)

Library of Congress Cataloging-in-Publication Data

Kilpatrick, Bob, 1952 –
        The art of being you : how to live as God's masterpiece / Bob Kilpatrick and Joel
    Kilpatrick.
            p.   cm.
        ISBN 978-0-310-32544-4 (hardcover, jacketed)
        1. God (Christianity). 2. Spirituality. 3. Christianity and art. I. Kilpatrick, Joel. II.
    Title.
    BT103.K4648   2010
    248.4 – dc22   2010020446

All Scripture quotations, unless otherwise indicated, are taken from the New King James Version®.
© 1982 by Thomas Nelson. Used by permission. All rights reserved. Scripture quotations marked NIV
are taken from The Holy Bible, New International Version®, NIV®. Copyright © 1973, 1978, 1984, 2011 by
Biblica, Inc.® Used by permission of Zondervan. All rights reserved worldwide. www.Zondervan.com.
"NIV" and "New International Version" are trademarks rergeigistered in the United States Patent and
Trademark Office by Biblica, Inc.® Scripture quotations marked MSG [or The Message] are taken from
The Message. Copyright © 1993, 1994, 1995, 1996, 2000, 2001, 2002. Used by permission of Tyndale
House Publishers, Inc.

Any Internet addresses (websites, blogs, etc.) and telephone numbers printed in this book
are offered as a resource. They are not intended in any way to be or imply an endorsement
by Zondervan, nor does Zondervan vouch for the content of these sites and numbers for
the life of this book.

Published in association with the literary agency of WordServe Literary Group, Ltd., 10152
S. Knoll Circle, Highlands Ranch, CO 80130.

Cover design: *Studio Gearbox*
Cover illustration: *© Illustration Works, Corbis*
Interior design: *Beth Shagene*

First printing March 2016 / Printed in the United States of America

For Cindy and Ana Maria

Great art is as irrational
as great music.
It is mad with its own loveliness.
George Jean Nathan, drama critic

God is really only another artist.
He invented the giraffe, the elephant,
and the cat. He has no real style.
He just goes on trying other things.
Pablo Picasso, painter

No great artist ever sees things as they really are.
If he did, he would cease to be an artist.
Oscar Wilde, playwright

For the mystic what is how.
For the craftsman how is what.
For the artist what and how are one.
William McElcheran, sculptor

The question of common sense is
what is it good for?—
a question which would abolish
the rose and be answered triumphantly
by the cabbage.
James Russell Lowell, poet

CONTENTS

CONTENTS

ART VS. MATH

Art is the triumph over chaos.

John Cheever, novelist

We laid my dad to rest in Arlington National Cemetery. A wagon carried his remains behind a riderless horse. Twenty-one guns cracked their salute; the chief of Air Force chaplains delivered a homily; and it was finished. That's when I really began to think about eternity. I had always *talked* of heaven and eternity, but now I had experienced something close and unexpected and painful.

My dad no longer had a mortgage, a marriage, a pain in his body, or a single worry about this life. The file marked August Christian Kilpatrick was closed forever. The finality hit me again and again. I saw all around me, and particularly in my own body, the signs of time passing. I was walking the same path my dad had just left, and it would end the same way. I would die, and my mortgage, marriage, pains, and worries would all be behind me. The file with my name on it would close.

In the meantime, why was I here? What was life for? What was God doing in me, and why?

I asked these questions, and many more. I read a lot of books and talked to my wife, children, and closest friends. Through these conversations—especially with my friend Rick Enloe—my understanding of God and his purposes was profoundly changed. Rick and I have been friends for twenty-five years, and our relationship lacks artifice. Friends like this talk differently than accountability partners, cell group members, fellow churchgoers, or minister buddies. We wouldn't know how to hide from each other even if we wanted to.

Rick and I spent many late nights talking on his deck in Gig Harbor, by the fire in my living room, under Shakespeare's Head on Carnaby Street in London, and looking out across the blue-green Mediterranean Sea in Vernazza, Italy. We talked especially about Dorothy L. Sayers' book *The Mind of the Maker*, and over time we came to a liberating and delightful conclusion:

God is not trying to solve the problems we call "ourselves."

He is not attempting to repair us. God is more than a mathematician or mechanic.

God is an artist. He is preparing the greatest art show ever staged, and we are the materials of his art, the grandest expression of his creativity. The art show he is preparing transcends canvas, clay, chords, or cinema. He has expressed his creativity in you and me and is making a living display out of the whole human race.

This precious truth, like the pearl of great price, can change our lives forever. Yet in the course of many conversations, it became clear that this way of understanding God goes against what many Christians think. I heard a well-known Christian musician say in a concert that God is in the business of fixing broken people. I went home and thought about that for a while, and I came to a different conclusion. I can't find anything in the Bible that says God wants to fix broken people. I don't think God wants to be known as the Great Mechanic who replaces faulty parts on otherwise good engines. He's out not to rebuild us but to remake us. God wants us *to die* and *to be resurrected*. He desires to lead us into new life, to make us new creations.

God looks at us as an artist does his favorite work of art.

Our perception of God—what we believe about God, what we think he is doing in our lives, and especially *why* we think he's doing it—will set the course of our lives. Too often, instead of enjoying the beauty our Maker is creating in and through us, we view God through the lens of our personal weakness. Our theology is shaped by what we *lack* rather than by *who God is*.

For example, if we see ourselves as a problem needing a solution, we want God to be a mathematician.

If we see ourselves as broken and needing repair, we want God to be a mechanic.

If we see ourselves as lonely, we want God to be a friend.

If we see ourselves as ignorant, we want God to be a teacher.

It's as if we are all lining up to visit the Wizard of Oz, each with our own deep deficiency, and the wizard becomes to each of us what we need.

God does meet our deepest needs in very personal ways, but seeing him through the prism of our own weakness keeps us from knowing and enjoying him in his fullness. It can be dangerous to our faith if our overriding goal is for God to meet our needs. Rather, our highest priority should be knowing who God is and what he is up to in our lives—and why.

Jesus illustrated the danger of misperceiving God with a parable about a master who entrusts funds to three of his servants to invest while he is away (Matthew 25:14–30). On his return, two of them had risked and won. The third servant, however, is the focus of the parable. He said to his master, "I knew you to be a hard man, reaping where you have not sown . . . . And I was afraid." This statement reveals that the servant knew the character of the master, just as the other two servants did, but perceived the master differently based on his own personal deficiency and fear.

The result was pretty bad. That's why it is important for us to have a correct perception of God's character and ultimate purpose for us.

A New Paradigm

If we focus on God making repairs to our broken lives, we miss what he is really doing in us. Math equates, but art creates. "If anyone is in Christ, he is a *new* creation; old things have passed away; behold, all things have become *new*!" (2 Corinthians 5:17, emphasis added).

Sometime early in my Christian life, I came to believe that I was a problem that needed to be solved. I spent many hours at many altars offering the enigmatic equation of my life to the Master Mathematician, hoping he would solve it and I would be happy. But over time I saw that my entire approach was wrong. Perhaps because I have spent my life as an artist, surrounded by colleagues, friends, and family members who are illustrators, painters, writers, designers, songwriters, musicians, and sculptors, I came to see that the math paradigm is hopelessly inadequate to describe and deal with the human condition or the purposes of God. We need a new paradigm.

Art, not math.

Artist, not mathematician.

What do I mean by these terms *math* and *art*? Let me give each a thumbnail description, but let me also say that these things are mysteries. Avant-garde musician Laurie Anderson once said, "Talking about art is like dancing about architecture." It can be useless to try to use one to explain the other. But let's dance around the definitions a bit to make them come alive. If I were sitting next to you now, I would ask you to read each item on the following list slowly and pause for a while to consider them. Maybe I should have written *Selah* after each line.

Math	Art
Math equates	*Art creates*
Math brings order out of chaos	*Art makes beauty out of the order*
Facts are Math	*Faith is Art*
Justice is Math	*Mercy is Art*
Law is Math	*Grace is Art*
Exchanges are Math	*Gifts are Art*
Hierarchy is Math	*Servanthood is Art*
Pride is Math	*Sacrifice is Art*
Evangelism is Math	*Friendship is Art*
Cell groups are Math	*Relationships are Art*
Accountability partners are Math	*True friends are Art*
Churchgoing is Math	*Fellowship is Art*
Prayer lists are Math	*Communion is Art*

Devotions are Math	*Devotion is Art*
Tithing is Math	*Generosity is Art*
Fear is Math	*Love is Art*

Everything in the math column has some sort of equation, comparison, or measurement to it—we measure our time, money, sins, souls, members, positions, and friends. Nothing in the art column does. Math keeps count, while art makes something new and often unexpected. What would you add to this list?

Some of my friends think I have included many good, godly things on the math side. Why, they ask, are prayer lists, accountability partners, cell groups, and tithing on this list? These are all good things, but they are not enough. I'm not against math—it's what keeps our houses and pants from falling down. Math brings order out of chaos.

But math is a created thing. Problem solving may appear to have creative aspects to it, but it is not essentially creative because it doesn't make something that never was before. It deals with facts and figures that are preexistent, observable, and measurable. Math doesn't create; it arranges.

You might think, "But I like math. I like to solve problems." So do I. But this book isn't about our personalities or abilities. I'm not asking how *you* see you; I'm asking how you think *God* sees you.

Do you think he sees you as his problem, or his canvas?

Is he your Solver, or your Savior?

Is he trying to fix you up, or make you new?

Math is perfectly suited for the physical universe. If ever God wanted to show us up close his mastery of engineering, chemistry, and design, it's in our own bodies. We are, as David says, "fearfully and wonderfully made" (Psalm 139:14). But we are more than the sum of our chemicals and proportions. We are spiritual—we think, feel, remember, hope, and create. These things are art, not math.

If the world was merely physical, math is all God would need. But the universe has an invisible, spiritual dimension where math just doesn't work. In this spiritual dimension, whose child is the physical realm, there is no gravity, space, or time. Everything seems to be inside out. To go up, one must go down. To be the greatest, one must be the least. The fools are wise, the weak are strong, the humble are exalted and, strangest of all, the ruler of it all is the servant of all!

CHOOSE YOUR ART METAPHOR

Maybe you don't like art. Maybe a discussion about paintings and songs and poems leaves you cold. Maybe you relate to something entirely different. Maybe you are reading this because your wife or mother or accountability partner insisted on it.

Here's a lifeline for you: You can choose your own art metaphor. See your life as a country music song, or a chainsaw sculpture, or a really good movie. See it as a glass blowing, ironwork, or crochet.

Maybe you like to think of your life as a short film. Or maybe it's a Broadway musical. Maybe it's a haiku: short and sweet. Or maybe you're an epic poem: long, but enthralling. Maybe you are an inspired engineering design for a bridge or building. God knows what kind of art you are, and it doesn't hurt to visualize yourself in terms you find favorable.

I asked a lawyer-friend of mine who is legal counsel to a state agency how his day had gone. He paused, then said, "Well, I wrote a brilliant explanation of a policy issue that immediately resolved a potentially thorny conflict that was headed to court." Then he gave a little contented chuckle. Perhaps you are like that—a well-crafted summation. The metaphor that communicates God's intentions for you is the one you should keep in mind.

YOU: THE MASTERPIECE

Art is creative. Art makes beauty beyond order. Artists make something that never was before. They tell a story. I can program a computer to take all the notes in the musical scale and arrange them in some order, but we wouldn't necessarily call it music and it wouldn't be something new. It would simply be the same notes in a different order.

But when Mozart combined the notes into his *Requiem*, we have musical art of enduring beauty that sublimely calls to some other part of us, beyond math.

God wants to tell a story in you—the Story *of* You—that is unlike any story ever before or to come. Ephesians 2:10 reads, "We are His workmanship, created in Christ Jesus for good works." The word *workmanship* in this verse used to put me in the mind of the Erector set I had as a boy, as though God were screwing us together like I used to do with my little Erector beams and bolts. But the Greek word used here is much more evocative than that. It is *poiema*, from which we get our word *poem*.

Our physical bodies may be God's Erector set, but our hearts and souls, dreams and passions—these are his poetry.

When John writes, "In the beginning was the Word, and the Word was God" (John 1:1), he reveals an expressive God, one who wants to stand on the stage of eternity and shout a poem to the universe—and that poem is you.

None of us is a paint-by-numbers kit. You are not a machine to be fixed or a problem to be solved and shelved. You are God's performance art. There is coming a day when he will gather all his art together, the curtains will open, the lights will come bursting on in all their brilliance—and the art show will begin. Here, in his earthly workshop, right now, he is preparing you for it.

God is calling you to the greatest adventure known to mankind—being a living work of art in the hands of the Master Artist. He calls you to place your life unreservedly in his skilled care, to trust him, to step outside the mathematical borders of your life and live beyond the equation. He can't wait to get started on you. He knows precisely what he wants to make out of you. You are a fresh canvas on which God intends to paint yet another masterpiece.

Let the art begin!

1

THE ART
OF BEING SAVED—
NOT SOLVED

Like "happiness," our two terms "problem"
and "solution" are not to be found in the Bible—
a point which gives to that wonderful literature
a singular charm and cogency.
L. P. Jacks, "Stevenson Lectures"

The concept of "problem and solution"
is as meaningless, applied to creation, as it is
when applied to the act of procreation. To add
John to Mary in a procreative process does
not produce a "solution" of John's and Mary's
combined problem; it produces George or Susan.
Dorothy L. Sayers, *The Mind of the Maker*

I have observed a common thread in the disappointments and failures of faith that many of my friends have experienced. They were expecting to receive from Jesus the perfect spiritual equation that would solve their problems and make them whole. Some of my friends called Jesus "the Answer," as though he were the neat resolution to every question. Many of these friends believed in promises that were never made to them—at least not by God.

One young airman I knew wanted out of the Air Force very badly. He believed God had spoken to him and that he would be released from the military on a specific date. When the date came and went without his miracle release, he quit Jesus in disgust, left our community of believers, and went AWOL.

Another close Christian friend once told me he struggled with thoughts of suicide. "But I know Christians aren't supposed to feel that way," he said. He imagined there was an equation for spiritual success that, if he could only find it, would make him not "feel that way." He had bought into the way of math, but the equation was failing in his own life. Thankfully, he never acted on those impulses. He eventually moved into a mature and artistic understanding of who God had called him to be.

If the Christian life were an equation — Problem + Solution = Happiness — we would have solved it long ago. But we haven't. All the self-help programs that advertise a better life in six easy steps, or thirty days to a new you, or ten habits that will change you forever are trying to solve the problem that you think you are. They are trying to grant you happiness through an equation.

Every testimony you've ever heard in church probably fits neatly into this equation too. "I had a problem. I found the solution. Now I'm happy." I have heard this equation voiced in thousands of ways in my life — at youth camps and testimony services and in small groups. We witness to people using the same equation. "You have a problem. If you accept the solution, you'll be happy." We try to convince people of the logic of our faith. We reason. We count up the evidence and offer up verdicts and conclusions. We add everything up, hoping the sum of it all will prove convincing to others and ourselves.

Math deals with the facts — assessing them, putting them in order, and coming to a conclusion that can be filed away once and for all in the "Solved" folder of our brains. This works great for numbers — nobody wakes up having to recalculate 3 + 3; that problem has been solved to everyone's satisfaction. But humans are not math problems. We don't get "solved" when we get saved — if we did, there would be no unhappy Christians. Problem + Solution = Happiness just doesn't work with anything dynamic and alive, such as you and me. As Dorothy Sayers makes clear in *The Mind of the Maker*, 1 + 1 does not always make 2. In terms of procreation, John + Mary equals something that never was before—a new life. This is how God works in us.

MATH AND ORDER

The impulse toward equation-based living probably comes from the human impulse toward order, which is not in itself a bad thing. From the beginning of time, man has wanted to bring order to his life and world. God knew this. He called on Adam to give names to the animals. When the earliest people cleared a spot to make a comfortable bed for the night, they were ordering their world. When they decided that a particular cave would be their home, they were making order. Words, language, numbers, laws, planting, reaping, cooking, stacking, folding, and trading are all ways of ordering.

But man has always reached beyond order for something more, something beautiful. Since the earliest cave drawings, we have decorated our living spaces with colors and designs that please us and tell a story. In this fundamental way, we are like God.

God is an artist. I'm not talking in some sentimental

"he painted the skies with his fingers, the sunsets with his heavenly brush" way. I can't imagine worshiping a God like this any more than you can. True art is never sentimental. Rather, God's entire approach to the universe and to your life is of a Master Artist toward his favorite piece of artwork. Look at how God characterizes himself in the Bible, and you can't get away from this fact. The very first verb in the Bible describes an artistic act:

"In the beginning God created ..."

God then moved joyfully and deliberately through a series of artistic actions that resemble any great artist in moments of inspiration. He divided the light from the darkness, formed the continents of the earth, imagined all manner of growing plant life, populated the land and air with an astounding diversity of creatures, filled the oceans with swimming things, and then brought all those ideas to their apex with a creature that could actually bear the image of God: mankind.

Anyone who has ever been caught up in inspiration over a new idea probably knows exactly how God felt during the creation.

The Bible goes on to testify that our God is an artist.

"We are the clay, and You our potter; and all we are the work of Your hand," said Isaiah (Isaiah 64:8).

"Did not He who made me in the womb make them? Did not the same One fashion us in the womb?" (Job 31:15).

"But no one says, 'Where is God my Maker, who gives songs in the night?'" (Job 35:10).

"When I consider Your heavens, the work of Your fingers ..." (Psalm 8:3).

"Your hands have made me and fashioned me" (Psalm 119:73).

We see God's artistry in the way he communicates with us throughout history. He is fond of using metaphors—word pictures—from everyday life. He called the Israelites his sheep, trees, clay, and flowers. He told Abraham that his seed would be like the stars in the sky and the grains of sand on the seashore. God's natural language is art.

God appeared to Moses in a bush that was on fire but was never consumed, perhaps the first surrealist art in recorded history. He gave wild, vivid, and bizarre visions and dreams to the prophets, which have always seemed to me like heavenly films with their own setting, actors, and narrative arc. Jesus communicated much of his message in parables, many of which began "The kingdom of heaven is like ..." He did not come as a master lawyer with the contracts drawn up that would save our souls, if only we signed on the dotted line. He did not come as a scientist to explain in laboratory terms what this transaction of salvation and regeneration would result in.

Rather, he presented himself as an artist, drawing imagery from everyday surroundings—vines, mountains, rivers, clouds, birds, flowers. He used fictional stories to reveal truth about the kingdom, making up characters ("There was a certain man ..."), settings, plots, and surprise endings. He weaved dramatic stories for his listeners, just as his Father had done throughout history and through the prophets.

Yes, God also gave laws and commandments. But those have always seemed to me to be the tools and materials for his art. It was as though God, in laying out certain rules, chose the various kinds of brushes and paints he would need for the project at hand and placed a certain canvas on the easel. All artists have a particular way of organizing their space, of approaching their work, and of setting up their artistic routines. The commandments and laws were like God's way of setting up his studio: "I will need these to make the kind of masterpieces I envision in these people."

Why did God do this? Why did he create music? Color? Taste? Sex? If he was merely interested in order, he could have left these things out and no one would have noticed. Pleasure and beauty would be missing, and we would be none the wiser.

But God loves art. He loves to make beautiful things, and he does so lavishly. Did you know there are more than twenty-five thousand different kinds of spiders? (One kind would have been enough for me, and no hairy legs.) God seems to get carried away with his ideas. He designs one spider with long legs and a pinpoint body, then another with short fuzzy legs and a huge (for a spider) body. There are bouncing spiders and leaping spiders and spitting spiders.

Why so many different spiders? It's another vivid example of how artistically boundless God is. He is full of creative ideas. Look around you at the people you see each day. All of them are made with the same basic design, yet each is unique. There are no two people alike, not even twins. People, animals, stars, flowers, mountains, sun, rain, and rivers all point to one thing—God is *crazy* creative.

Why, then, when we think about God's relationship to us, do we hesitate to follow God into art? Why do we see God as merely wanting to solve us, organize us, and conform us? Our perception of God is not so much skewed as it is incomplete. We have come to the math of God, stopped, and built our cities there. We have failed to see the same sort of boundless creativity and delight he displays in the creation of spiders expressed in the care and attention he gives to developing our eternal selves. Jesus told us he was going to prepare a place for us in heaven. But heaven is not God's "Solved Forever" folder. It is not a stopping place; it's a starting place. Earth is God's art studio, and heaven is his showplace.

HOW GOD SEES YOU

If we think of life as math, we end up counting rather than creating. We believe in an Accountant God who keeps strict ledgers and is mainly concerned with counting our sins. What we sing about Santa, we really believe about God:

> *He's making a list*
> *and checking it twice*
> *Gonna find out who's naughty and nice*
> *Santa Claus is comin' to town*
> *He sees you when you're sleeping*
> *He knows when you're awake*
> *He knows if you've been bad or good*
> *So be good for goodness sake*

We believe in a God of math. God is always counting, and there is surely more in the debit column than in the credit column of our lives. Come judgment day we are going to be in a whole heap of trouble.

Yet God didn't solve us—he saved us. We are his art. He has thrown us on the wheel and wrapped his hands around the wet clay of our lives. He redeemed us so he could remake us. Art doesn't count; it *creates*. When Jesus gave himself for us on the cross, he wasn't meeting our cosmic debt to the last penny, like some bean-counting miser. He was doing that spider thing again. He was creating. He went so far beyond our debt—so extravagantly does he value us—that he lifted us right out of the equation. He more than met the obligation, brought the debit column to way past zero, and elevated us into art.

The crucifixion is where his mercy moved from the conceptual to the real, from the abstract to the concrete, from thought to action. It is where God's ultimate artistic vision became present in human history. To be real, art must be expressed in a tangible way in a moment of time. There is no such thing as an unpainted painting, an unsung song, an unwritten novel. It may reside in the mind of the artist, but to become art and to have the power of art, it must come into existence. That is what happened at the cross. Its power and beauty stem from the fact that the crucifixion occurred in space and time: there was a desolate hill called Golgotha outside a city called Jerusalem; there was a betrayal by a close follower and friend; there was the judgment of an innocent person at the hands of a diffident governor; his hands and feet were pierced by rough nails that pinned him to a cross; he hung between two thieves; and there he died.

These are more than facts; they are the window through which we see the art of God on display to all his creation. The crucifixion of Jesus is art at its highest and most creative.

ART AND MYSTERY

Somewhere along the line, Christians began to expect the Bible to be more like a textbook than an expression of the art and mystery of God. Mystery has been so banished from Protestant churches that most of them have adopted theologies that more or less leave the mystical completely out of their practices. Today the Protestant Church is by and large disengaged from any true artistic or mystical expression of the faith.

Oh, we use the arts, especially music and drama, as vehicles to communicate our beliefs, but we use them to argue a point rather than tell a story. We tell the facts as though they were the whole truth. We reason rather than point to the mystery. We speak to the mind rather than to the heart. We use artistic tools in mathematical ways, which is why so much of our church-based "art" is hollow and thin. It's not even art. It's an ad campaign. It's logic masquerading as mystery.

Think about the spiritual advertising that passes as evangelism these days. We're offering nonbelievers a "product" that will enhance the enjoyment of life and eternity. Our T-shirts become billboards. (My daughter wanted to print one that proclaimed "They will know we are Christians by our T-shirts.") Our songs and plays are like infomercials. "Find the solution to your problem and be happy in Jesus! Your life will be better! But wait!

There's more! Your eternity will be better too!" I have long thought that some Christians, perhaps in a desperate attempt to "sell" more of the gospel product, have a tendency to claim things about the gospel that they know to be untrue. The further we step into sales and marketing, the further away we get from the power and truth of art.

For a time in the eighties and nineties it was popular among youth groups on mission trips to perform mimes to Christian songs. Some denominations even had "human video" contests at youth conventions and fine arts festivals, as if this were its own category of art right alongside painting and poetry. I remember seeing Carmen's song "The Champion" mimed about a thousand times by youth groups from Albuquerque to Albany. I have to credit them for their consistency. Most of their "performances" included the same types of garish, grimacing demons in black jeans and T-shirts flailing and slinking around an effete, silent Jesus figure clad all in white. Perhaps without knowing it, they were actually reviving an old tradition of morality plays of the Middle Ages, in which the eternal struggle between God and Satan for the souls of humans was played out by archetypal characters. An evangelistic tract in narrative form, yes. Scripturally defensible, perhaps. Interesting, sometimes (but in most cases not for the reasons they wanted it to be). Art, no.

Thankfully, it has been years since I saw "The Champion" mimed by any youth groups. Now YouTube is the communication vehicle of choice for Christians with dramatic tendencies. Recently I saw a video on the Internet put out by one of the leading "emerging" church pastors. It was well produced and carefully thought-out, featuring a musical metaphor for the message of the gospel. It struck me, though, how inartistic it was in its core. When all the "art" was stripped away it was not really art at all but a rational presentation of the claims of Christ—a form of reason and debate. For all its artistic dressing it was still an attempt at winning the theological argument. Again, logic dressed up as mystery.

Perhaps we don't like mystery because mystery seems to be God's way of getting us to surrender. If there were no mystery, we might try to do God's work for him. One of my friends said, "If I can understand it, I can manage it; and if I can manage it, I can control the outcome." This seems to be the goal of some Christians: to fully understand God so they can control the outcome. But control is not the goal of art—the goal is mystery and surrender.

In Ephesians 3:9, Paul refers to us as the "fellowship of the mystery." Writing to Timothy in his first letter he tells his young protégé "great is the mystery of godliness" (1 Timothy 3:16). Paul and Jesus both talk about the mysteries of the kingdom of God. As a contrast, the concept of "winning" anyone to Jesus is mentioned only once— and almost in passing—by Peter in his advice to women married to unbelieving husbands; and he says it should be done "without a word" (1 Peter 3:1). This brings to mind the well-known saying widely attributed to Saint Francis: "Preach the gospel at all times, and if necessary, use words."

Why does "winning" loom so large in our modern theology, while the idea of holy mystery is nearly anathema? Is it because "souls saved" can be counted (math), but mysteries (art) cannot? As a result of our emphasis on logic and winning, we have reversed the proper order and made art serve math. We sing and act and write and paint and make films *only to save souls.* It's another example of an ad campaign — a noble one, but still an ad campaign.

Using the arts is easy, but few of us *live* as art. We have forgotten somehow that God is a creative being in every wonderful sense of the word. He created us to live outside the equation, in art. Saint Irenaeus declared, "The glory of God is man fully alive." That's what God wants for us. We're always trying to add it up, but God wants us to *live* it up.

Math Christians don't like this idea. They don't like the mystery of God. They want evidence and a verdict. They like to point out that Jesus said we will be judged by every idle word we speak (Matthew 12:36). Doesn't that sound like a threat to you? Every word you have ever spoken is on heaven's record — so you'd better watch out.

I can't help but imagine myself on judgment day standing before a crowd of people, every one of them watching as my private life is projected on a screen for all to see. There I am in the bathroom; there I am a stupid teenager; there I am snoring. Oh, this looks fun! Sinatra sang, "Forget your troubles, come on get happy, . . . get ready for the judgment day." Get happy?! What's to be happy about?

But now look at that "every idle word" quote through a different lens—the lens of art. Instead of threatening us with Big Brother surveillance, it seems to me that Jesus is simply saying that our true character comes out in the unguarded words we speak, not in the words we say for show. He is reminding us that it's not the pre- pared speeches and everyday conversational courtesies that reveal us, but the words we say straight from the heart. When anybody wants to find out what you are really made of, they listen there.

This is God being an artist. Every artist wants to know what materials he has to deal with when creating art. He can't pretend he's working with plaster when it's really papier-mâché. Before a musician plays an instrument, he picks it up and strums or bows it and gets a sense of the tone and range. What is the true timbre of the thing? He has to know before he can make music with it. In the same way, a potter can't pretend that the clay is pure and will hold up in the kiln when it's not. He must know the material.

I have a dozen or so guitars hanging on the walls of my recording studio. Each one of them has a different sound. When I'm recording, I will play each of them and find the one that fits the song I'm working on. None of them fits every tune, but all of them have their unique place.

So God is looking at the real you, not the "show you." He's listening for what you're made of. Eugene Peterson says we go through life imitating ourselves. We play the best version of us — but God pays no attention to our act. He's listening for the unguarded words, the thoughts and intentions of the heart, and he's seeking to discover what we are really made of because he wants to know the true material he's working with.

This is not a threat; it's an artistic assessment by the Artist himself.

GOD'S TOOLS?

Because mystery is so unsettling, many of us choose to think of ourselves primarily as tools in the hands of God. We want to be used to build or fix things, to impact and change the world — a practical purpose.

God does have a purpose for each one of us here, a job for us to undertake, some responsibilities that give us fulfillment. The first words God said to Adam and Eve in Genesis 1:28 commissioned them for a duty: "Be fruitful and multiply; fill the earth and subdue it; have dominion over the fish of the sea, over the birds of the air, and over every living thing that moves on the earth."

But many of us see ourselves *only* as a tool in the hands of God. Our identity becomes too tightly defined by our earthly purpose and tasks. We forget that every earthly responsibility is an exercise in terminal duty. No one is going to ask you in heaven, "So, what do you do?" or even, "So, what did you do?" There is no need in eternity for plumbers, electricians, salesmen, writers, soldiers, homemakers, fathers, mothers, or politicians. Equally, there is no heavenly duty for the apostle, prophet, evangelist, pastor, or teacher. The Bible does indicate we will have responsibilities in eternity, but we are not given much information as to what shape they will take.

Rather than seeing you primarily as his tool, God views your purpose here as a tool in his hands for the art he is making of you. He is at work *in* you more than *through* you, shaping you through the things you do, the people you meet, and the circumstances of your life. While we are busy going about our purpose, God is busy going about his—to conform you to the image of his Son; to display his exquisite gracefulness through you in eternity; to make of you a creative expression, his *poiema*.

While we are thinking of our purpose here on earth, God is considering our eternal purpose.

When I first realized this, it was as if my world suddenly turned inside out. It was like looking at one of those optical illusions where you see a grizzled old hag if you look at it one way and a beautiful young woman if you look at it another. Up to that point, I had seen myself as a tool in the hands of God—a useful one, I hoped. He had hold of me and was using me to change the world in some small way. But when my perspective changed, the image changed and reversed. I was still in God's hands, but rather than using me as a tool, it was as though I was a piece of wood being turned on a lathe. I had thought I was the chisel, but then I saw I was the stone. He was using the circumstances of my life to chip and grind against me, to form me into his art. I wasn't the tool anymore; I was the masterpiece-in-progress. This was a profound change in my perspective.

Some people get this. A well-known evangelist once told me, "It's a good thing God called me to this ministry. I need to be in church, in this atmosphere, all the time." He had a rare insight into what God was doing in him, which was to use his calling and placement as an instrument to work his art in him. And this is what God is doing in each and every one of us. He is at work in a completely other, deeper, more mysterious way in our lives.

While we consider ourselves as tools to be used on some project, in God's eyes, we *are* the project. He is using our very responsibilities to form and shape us.

None of us is merely a tool in God's hands. You are not an equation or an accounting error that God may get around to solving one day—if you pray hard enough. You are the material of his art. And he saved you because he delights in expressing his creativity through you.

Let's see how.

2

ART AND ANTI-ART

In art, and in the higher ranges of science,
there is a feeling of harmony which underlies all
endeavor. There is no true greatness in art
or science without that sense of harmony.
Albert Einstein

Oh I do want that thing, that oneness
of movement that will catch the thing up into
one movement and sing—harmony of life.
Emily Carr, twentieth-century painter

Art has no end but its own perfection.
Plato

Years ago, I was singing for two nights in a church on Chicago's south side. After the first concert, a young lady introduced herself and asked me to pray with her. She shared her need—I think it was for more of God and more money. I held her hands, and we prayed. I was at the church again the next night, and so was she. This time she had dressed up considerably and put some eau de parfum to injudicious use. She approached me after the concert with a slip of paper. On it was her address and phone number. She invited me over for a late dinner. When I suggested that the pastor already had dinner plans for me, she invited me to stop in any time I was in Chicago; and if I needed a place to stay, I was welcome to bunk down at her place. In fact, if my hotel was lonely, I was welcome to come over that night. I kindly told her that I would never be doing any such thing.

I thought I was no longer a candidate for come-ons. After all, I'm bald, I'm married, and I have children and grandchildren. And what self-respecting Christian woman goes to church expecting to hit on the guest minister?

But sin is pervasive and sometimes, as in this case, blind. We can't *solve* sin. There is no solution waiting

to be discovered that will subtract sin from the human
equation forever. Sin is not a puzzle or a math problem.
Rather, it's like shower mold. You clean it thoroughly,
and it immediately starts growing and spreading again.
It's dynamic, not static.

I wish I had understood this earlier. I have repented
to God for virtually the same set of sins my whole life.
Early on in the process, I figured God must be awfully
irritated with me for not staying clean. I thought many
times that he was probably getting ready to set me aside
or throw me away.

But God doesn't see our sin as a problem to be solved
any more than he sees our lives as problems to be solved.
Sin is not botching the perfect equation; sin is messing
with God's art. It is the resistance of the living clay to
the hands of the Potter. Sin is whatever keeps the artist
from satisfying the vision he has for his piece. Sin is that
disunity and fragmentation of purpose that destroys a
work of art before it is ever complete. God wants us to
be free from sin because he knows what we can be without it. Every sin in our lives hinders his artistic pursuit
and keeps him from fulfilling that one pure, exalted,
and unique expression of creativity that he has in mind
for us.

Like all great artists, God is a perfectionist. We
wouldn't expect anything else. A filmmaker who willingly allows a mediocre performance to remain in his

film would betray his own art. God hates every sin because it is a flaw, however small, in his art.

We get the mistaken impression, however, that fixing these flaws is up to us. But paintings don't paint themselves or achieve perfection by somehow applying the pigment to their own canvas. It is the artist who will perfect the art. God will make of us what we should be. Our first and highest calling is to surrender to his artistic vision. God doesn't demand that we rid ourselves of sin. That is math. Instead, he calls us to lay down our arms and cease the resistance. That is all we can do.

ART AND HOLINESS

Put on your critic's cap and consider with me: What does an art critic or art lover look or listen for when judging a work of art? Shock value? Novelty? Brilliance? Profundity? Not really. Primarily we look for an internal logic, a consistency born of a single vision. The art must be true *to itself* to be true at all. Whether it's a song, painting, film, dance, poem, or book, all the parts must work together to tell one story.

I often tell aspiring songwriters that they should say one thing in their songs. If they try to say more than one thing, the power of the song diminishes considerably. As Søren Kierkegaard wrote, "Purity of heart is to will one thing."[1]

Deuteronomy 6:4 confirms this when it reads, "The
LORD is one!"

In Psalm 86:11, David said, "Unite my heart to fear
Your name."

Jesus said, "If therefore thine eye be single, thy whole
body shall be full of light" (Matthew 6:22 KJV).

James said that a double-minded man is unstable in all
his ways (James 1:8).

Unity is a big deal to God. Sin causes disunity. Sin
disrupts art. The power of your life, as God's work of
art, is in its unity and cohesion to a single vision. The
more fragmented or marred by sin the less powerful and
beautiful your artistic impact. God is at work in you to
make you one.

This is what the Bible means by holiness. When we
say God is holy, it means that he is full and complete
in himself, lacking nothing. Every artist strives to create
something unified and full of light. The best composi-
tions of Bach and Beethoven captivate us by their expert
craft, unity, and internal symmetry. All great art, from
Shakespeare to Rembrandt, does the same.

When the Bible tells us that we are to be holy as God
is holy, maybe you (like me) imagine severe ladies with
their hair pulled back in tight buns and men in ill-fitting
suits and bad haircuts—all clutching large Bibles and
frowning at the world. Clearly, holiness has some really
bad PR.

But this is not the holiness the Bible speaks of. It is, instead, our own attempts to be holy through math, to achieve artistic unity by way of an equation. We quit bad habits and make new good ones. We have devotions, read our Bibles, go to church services, do good works, and evangelize. We look around at what other Christians are doing and copy them.

When I was seventeen, I moved into a house ministry in northern California and went with the other guys there to the nearby Assemblies of God church, a rambunctious little fellowship on the edge of town. I remember Sister Decker and Brother Kern screwing up their faces into intense grimaces when they prayed, so I screwed up my face when I prayed too.

The dear saints there would also get a warble in their voices when they prayed. They would accent their prayers by waving one hand like a spiritual karate chop. They had a unique way of saying "Glory!" that made these Californians sound very Southern. I can still say it just the way they did: Glow-ree.

One Sunday morning, we had a long and passionate altar service. I prayed so hard for so long that I got a cramp in my face. But I still couldn't keep up with the pros. The other young people kneeling at the altar benches seemed so spiritual, while I was so messed up. I was wondering what the girl next to me looked like naked. I was wishing I could make up some great testimony that would impress all these people. I was tremendously jealous of the spiritual guys who sang and preached. I knew that if they knew who I really was, they would never let me in the cool club.

I'm pretty sure I could have kept living that way if I had been willing to keep faking it. There were plenty of examples around me of people doing that. There was the flashy evangelist in a three-piece suit and perfect hair who held a citywide crusade and saved a load of souls before getting caught doing some really bad things.

There was the other guy praying with me at the altar who ended up getting the girl next to me pregnant. There was the board member who could go from warbling prayer to vulgarity and back again without seeming to descend from glory.

But I actually believed that it was supposed to work; I just couldn't get it to. I guess I was looking for a new part for my broken spiritual motor. One pastor ended every sermon with, "I can see I'm not going to finish this sermon, but all I can say is, God will pull you through if you can stand the pullin'."

"That's it?!" I thought. "I'm supposed to screw up my face and try to stand the pullin'?!" One day all the warble went out of my praying voice; all the karate chop accents seemed futile and ridiculous. I was trying so hard, and I was running out of energy for it. "This is too hard," I thought. "I give up."

I was aiming at holiness but only succeeding at tying myself in religious knots.

I wish I had understood then what holiness was. The phrase "partakers of His holiness" in Hebrews 12:10 shows us God's intention to create in us the same internal logic and unity of truth that he enjoys and has put in all his creation. As the artist cannot help but be revealed in his art, so God's unity of being—his holiness—will be created in us and become the mark that we are his.

David wrote that we are to worship the Lord in the "beauty of holiness" (Psalm 29:2). Beauty? In holiness? When we see holiness in the light of art, it is not some quaint, legalistic idea; it is God's artistic vision. It isn't about making sure you've been nice and not naughty. God's idea of holiness is unity of artistic expression, and he is determined for you to embody that unity.

My wife, Cindy, and I had the opportunity to see a series of studies in charcoal that Picasso did in preparation for a drawing he had conceived. The progression of his idea over eighteen pieces of paper was remarkable. Each showed how he was developing the idea and wrestling with the vision until he had achieved the unity he sought. He could not have stopped at any of these intermediary drawings and called it a finished work. He was going for holiness.

So God has an artistic vision for each of us that he is working through to completion. He will not be satisfied until it is fulfilled. He wants us to be holy—full and complete, lacking nothing. Like the first verse of Psalm 23 declares: "GOD, my shepherd! I don't need a thing" (MSG).

I loved the Beatle song "Blackbird" from the very first time I heard it. It was the first pseudoclassical finger-picking song I actually learned to play. If you're familiar with the song, you know that it includes the lyrics, "Blackbird singing in the dead of night, take these broken wings and learn to fly," and later, "Take these sunken eyes and learn to see." As beautiful as the song is in both melody and poetry, there is no sense of uplift or redemption to it. It remains bleak from start to finish. So one day I decided to write another verse for it so I could help that broken bird find redemption and wholeness. I recorded the song on a live album, singing the original song and ending with my verse.

That turned out to be a big mistake. Shortly after my album came out, I got a letter from the Beatles' music company informing me that they were going to sue me. I had messed with their art, and they didn't like it one bit. For a true Beatle fan, this was a shocking and terrifying situation to be in. Not only that, but I saw the vast resources of the Apple Records empire coming down the track at me. I did the only thing I could—I begged, groveled, and pleaded ignorance. Wonder of wonders, they let me off the hook with an agreement that I wasn't allowed to reproduce any more of the records than were already manufactured (which is why there were only fifteen hundred copies of the album *It's Not Enough* ever made). I was utterly relieved not to be meeting the Fabs or their lawyers in court.

I understood their point of view more clearly when, a few years later, I had the same thing happen to me. An enterprising and eager Christian musician rewrote my song "Lord, Be Glorified," changing my words and melody slightly and adding what he thought were even better ideas. He then claimed a copyright on it and listed me as a cowriter. When I noticed this on a royalty statement from ASCAP, I found the guy, heard the song (it was terrible), and told him we had a problem. He was as terrified as I had been. I was as firm and kind with him as Apple Records had been with me, and you will not find his version of that song commercially available anymore.

The reason both the Beatles and I would not allow any changes to our songs is simply that we didn't want anyone else messing with the artistic unity of it. I get the impression that God feels the same way about us.

SINS OF
ARTISTIC OMISSION

If I had gone home with the woman in Chicago, it would have been like taking a knife and slashing the canvas

of my life or covering the emerging portrait with layers
of black paint. My ministry would have vanished, and
maybe my family and friends as well. Ripped canvases
can be repaired, certainly, but how much better not to
damage it in the first place.

But sin also can involve our not doing anything wrong
but rather withholding or resisting the right thing. This
has long been known as a sin of omission. Paul states that
knowing good and not doing it is sin (Romans 7:15–20).
Every artist knows instinctively what this means. If there
is a better lyric or melody that can be composed and you
don't do it, it is sin. If you could write more crisply and
you don't, it is sin. You are working against the good of
the art.

I was writing a song with a fellow musician a few years
ago. I had already written the verses and chorus alone,
and he and I were crafting a bridge of four lines to complete the song. We got through two lines rather easily,
but the last two were puzzling us. We spent the bulk of
the afternoon wrestling with words and trying various
lines. I'm sure he was a little frustrated with me because
I had some idea in my mind for a turn of phrase that was
elegant, simple, and better than what we had.

Cindy had called us, and our dinner was getting cold,
but I couldn't let it go. Suddenly, in a little geyser of creativity, it came to us.

> *Life's a mystery*
> *We don't always see God's hand*
> *He's the Lord of love and wonder*
> *One day we will understand*

I am vain enough to take foolish pride in those lyrics and tripping internal rhymes, but I could not have lived with the song or ever performed it if we hadn't persevered and come up with the last two lines. It would have been a sin.

On the other hand, while writing with another song-writer in Nashville, he introduced what I thought was an inferior lyric idea. I said that I thought we could do better. We moved on, but after a while, he brought the lyric back out again and would not let it go. We finished the song with the mediocre lyric in it, and he went on to record it, but I lost all interest in the song. In my opinion it was not good work and was not well done. It was sin.

The wonderful thing is that God hates our sin without hating us. He is an artist. Artists may hate whatever stands in the way of making great art, but they don't ever hate their art. I have never hated a song I wrote. I may have been frustrated by it, or I may have failed to realize the full artistic vision of it, but I never hated it. So God does not hate you. He loves you without fail. He is always looking forward to expressing himself in new and fuller ways through you. He is always bringing about a greater unity in your life so that his artistic vision comes closer to completion.

FORGIVENESS AS ART

Sin needs forgiveness. When God forgives sin, he provides the only remedy for it. Forgiveness is some of the best art there is. It is infinite. It cannot be accounted for. It messes up the justice equation so badly as to render it useless. Forgiveness is not the solution to a problem—it is not God adding a nickel back to your account after you commit a nickel's worth of sin. Rather, it is dynamic, powerful, and creative. It adds something that was not there before. Look at the etymology of the word. It comes from the Old English "to give for." Forgiving is the most creative act you or anyone can possibly perform. When you forgive someone, you give *for* them, obliterating the debit/credit count of sins and the math of guilt. Forgiveness says, "Your sins are remembered against you no longer." To forgive is art, and God uses art to set captive people free.

Excuses are math. They presuppose that justice is on our side. An excuse doesn't need to be forgiven; it only needs to be explained and understood. Excuses are the way we blame God—"You made me this way"—to disclaim responsibility. When we do, we forgo the art of forgiveness.

Some people play the role of the victim all their lives. Every act they do has a cause outside of themselves—their parents, the government, the boss, the wife, the husband, the kids, the economy, God. They feel as though they are forced to make the bad decisions they make, and therefore they are not to blame. When my children would fall into this devilish trap, I would have them repeat two things to me:

"I am not a victim."

"Circumstances do not hold ultimate power over me."

I was trying to reinforce in them a sense of responsibility for their own lives and decisions. I did this not to increase their load of guilt but to show them the only way out from under that load. If you are not responsible for your actions, God says, then bring me the person who is, and I will forgive them. Making excuses, blaming others, harboring a feeling of resentment at the way we were made—all these things leave us terribly burdened with guilt. Accepting the responsibility for our actions and giving them to God to be forgiven is the only way to freedom. No person is fundamentally a victim.

Promises of payback are also math, as is blaming others. But the apostle John states that if we confess our sins—that is, if we recognize those things that compromise

God's art in us—God is faithful and just to forgive us (1 John 1:9). He scrapes it off the canvas. He then cleanses us from all unrighteousness and begins anew to paint his masterpiece in us.

Many centuries ago, in the work yard of a cathedral in Florence, Italy, there stood a huge piece of white marble, eighteen feet high and weighing several tons. A sculptor had begun work on it, then abandoned it because it had what he considered a fatal flaw. It was such a massive block that all the artists of the city were aware of it. They called it *The Giant*. Many, including Leonardo da Vinci, wanted to get their hands on it. But the cathedral's Board of Works had not approved any of their plans. They seemed to realize the potential of this huge, intimidating piece of stone in the right artist's hands.

The stone sat untouched for thirty-five years. Then one day, a young sculptor named Michelangelo Buonarroti learned that the cathedral was finally ready to offer it to an artist. Leonardo da Vinci was a clear front-runner, as was another sculptor of the day who was lobbying hard to get it. Michelangelo hurried back to Florence from Rome and presented his idea for the marble block. The cathedral Board liked it, and he was commissioned to transform *The Giant* into a work of art.

Michelangelo chose the Bible's David as his subject, and from that marble—which had been worked on and abandoned by another artist and coveted by countless artists over the decades—he created the nearly seventeen-foot statue that looms grandly over art history. The *David* was so important, in fact, that art historians mark this as the start of the High Renaissance period.[2]

Interestingly, Michelangelo did not start the work on that marble block; another sculptor did decades earlier. But Michelangelo finished it with a completely new vision for what it could become. He even worked around the errors the previous sculptor had made in the stone.

Sometimes we think we are not good material for God to work with. We've been wrongly handled or feel fatally flawed. We can't picture ourselves becoming great works of art. But God knows better. He chose each of us out of the work yard and redeemed us for his pleasure. He can take any life that seems lost and misspent and redeem it. His creative vision for your life can still be realized, even after much destruction and pain.

We are meant to be beautiful—and we will be, in God's hands. Our enemy would like us to keep believing in equations. Satan loves math because when we calculate the value of our lives, we always come up short.

But God doesn't measure us that way. As with all art connoisseurs, the worth of his art is in the price he is willing to pay for it. He gave the very life of his Son to redeem and remake us! That means each of us is worth redeeming. I love the Gloria Gaither lyric: "All I had to offer Him was brokenness and strife, but He made something beautiful of my life."

God can make of us art so wonderful that it scarcely seems possible. Instead of solving us, God is preparing to create the art that we are meant to be.

3

THE ART OF LOVING RELATIONSHIPS

You cannot possibly invent painting
all by yourself.
Pierre Bonnard, French painter

Gauguin says that when sailors have to
move a heavy load or raise an anchor,
they all sing together to keep them up and give
them vim. That's just what artists lack!
Vincent van Gogh

In junior high at Brooks Air Station in San Antonio, Texas, I desperately wanted to be cool, and for a while I belonged to a cool group of boys. We hung around together, looked out for each other, and sat together on the wide backseat of the bus on our way to Harry H. Rogers School. Each day we would assign one boy to wait at the first bus stop to claim the seat for the rest of us.

One morning I climbed aboard and made my way to the back of the bus. But when I got close, none of the boys moved to make room for me. Then one of them spoke up. "We took a vote and decided that you aren't in the club anymore."

I hadn't seen this coming. I instantly felt like I was going to throw up. I sat down somewhere else and tried to be a man and not cry, looking out the window in case I did. A few stops later, my best buddy, Doug, got on the bus. When he reached me he got this quizzical look on his face and asked, "Why aren't you sitting at the back?"

"They don't want me in the club anymore," I said. It hurt to hear myself say it.

To my surprise, Doug dropped down into the seat next to me. "Well, if they don't want you, they don't want me either! We'll start our own club."

I wiped my eyes and said, "Yeah!"

The rest of the ride to school was magical. I could not believe what Doug had done, and I loved him for it. He gave up his own coolness for me. The other boys had counted—and I had lost. But Doug had created something new—our own club. By the end of the day, the other group had fallen apart, and all the boys joined us in our new club. Love conquers all!

THE BODY OF CHRIST
AS ART

I'm not sure if you have ever experienced an act of friendship like that, but the fact that I still look back on that day with great gratitude and deep feeling tells me just how powerful such an act can be. To be honest, I was disappointed to go through life and learn how rare such acts, and such people, are. Friendship can be difficult to come by. Unfortunately, this is even true within the body of Christ—but it doesn't have to be that way.

As Christians, we know we are supposed to be part of a loving community. We long for the closeness of Paul and Silas, of Jesus' disciples, of David and Jonathan. We want the bond that the early church had in the book of Acts. We want to be the body of Christ, but often math gets in the way. We begin friendships in some artless way, and then we expect them to operate well based on the equations of a "successful" community of believers. This often leads to disappointment, unmet expectations, shallow relationships, alienation, and even bitter separations.

The antidote to bad relationships is to see community as part of God's artistic expression. We must see relationships the way our Artist does—as vital to the work he is doing in each of us. Relationships give the art of our lives context and purpose. Think of your church or fellowship as a symphony orchestra. There are dozens of different instruments playing. The violins and the violas sweetly bow the melody; the trumpets come blaring in now and again; and the cymbals crash during the climactic sections. The bassoons sit off to the side, underlining the melody at key points. The flutes and piccolos flutter around like birds in the rafters. The conductor's job is to keep it all in rhythm and balance. Each player is an artist unto himself, yet each player subsumes his talent into the common vision of a single artist—the composer.

The beautiful thing about art, whether it be a symphony or a novel, is how the parts coalesce to make a powerful whole under the expert direction of the creator. Indeed, separately, each part would be greatly diminished, perhaps even unpleasing or nonsensical. When producing an album in the recording studio, I often take a moment to "solo" each part, meaning I listen to it without the rest of the instruments. Alone, each part can sound odd, out of place, or jarring. But what matters is that it sounds good in the context of the song.

The big picture of our lives, and of history, is God's intention to create the ultimate community of humanity, using as his materials those who know Jesus Christ. Relationships are foundational to his artwork. In fact, "Who do you know?" is the determining question of eternity.

The wonderful thing is that community does not mean conformity. This is a commonly expressed sentiment— one I'm sure you've heard before—but it bears repeating: there is no master mold that God is waiting to put you into so you can pop out as a replica of the person sitting next to you in the pew. The conformity to God's vision must be taken artistically; it is conformity to a larger purpose, not to each other.

When an artist wrestles with an idea, he rarely explores or fully exposits it in just one work. Rather, if he is a musician, he might make several albums in the same style or make one album whose songs are held together by a unifying concept. A painter will make a series of similar paintings, and playwrights will write a cycle on a theme. Any idea worth exploring is always too big for just one song, one painting, or one play. It has to be broken down into various facets to be fully realized. This is how artists work. They process through an idea over many individual expressions of it. Taken alone, each work is good; but taken together as a series, each part gains fuller meaning as we see it in relation to the bigger idea being explored. So it is with Christian community. Each one of us is a work of art; but together, we tell an even greater story.

In my living room I have a papier-mâché work of art —a large, cartoonish blowfish titled "Pez Bola," by the Mexican artist Sergio Bustamante. On top is his signature followed by the letters "AP," which stand for *artist's proof.* As he worked out his vision for this piece, this was the one that he loved the most and felt expressed his ideal. He then used it as the model for all the rest in the series. Jesus, too, is the artist's proof, the first in the series, the one whom God most loved and felt expressed his ideal. In Romans 8:29, Paul calls Jesus the "firstborn among many." Paul says earlier in the same verse that we are to be conformed to the image of Jesus. In God's earthly workshop, he is creating the rest of the series in this artistic vision—that's you and me. We are not the single expressions of God's idea. We are part of an artistic series, a mosaic—the body of Christ.

FRIENDSHIPS AS ART

Friendship is not the result of an equation any more than priceless art can be created by a computer program. It's a shame, then, that instead of allowing the art of friendship to flourish, many churches have turned friendship into math. Instead of authentic bonds of friendship and love, we have created things like ... accountability partners.

It may just be that I'm a contrarian, but I have always thought that an accountability partner is a poor stand-in for a true friend. It's such a mechanical, robotlike construction. It has math written all over it. Do we think that we can in some religious laboratory bring to life that natural attraction and fellowship with each other that springs from the Spirit? In my experience, such attempts usually result in Franken-friends—synthetic relationships that horrify rather than edify.

God wants us to have friends. Jesus enjoyed and needed the friendship of his disciples. But does God want our friendships to be created artificially by a church group? I heard of a couple who attended a cell group in their church for ten years. One evening they told the group that they would no longer be coming because they were getting a divorce. No one in the group had an inkling that this couple was having marriage troubles! When we have been organized and slotted into "relationships" like this, we bring only what we want to bring. We might tell of our petty trials and yet be silent about our deepest struggles.

God's church is organic, not mechanical. It is the body of Christ, made alive and held together by that which every joint supplies, not bolted together like machined metal. God, keep us from building Erector-set churches!

When Cindy and I were a young married couple, we and a few friends from church decided to start meeting in our homes every Friday night to discuss the Bible. The group flourished. We met for more than ten years, and some of the best learning and best conversations I have ever had happened in those meetings. We rotated homes and invited other friends. Four or five couples formed the unchanging nucleus of the group, and others passed in and out over time. The relationships forged during that time are some of the strongest that I have.

After a decade, our church decided to move into "cell group ministry" and create groups to meet in the various parts of town. We were asked by administrators at the church to come under the umbrella of this new church-wide effort. The church began feeding people into our group by geographical location, and our group became answerable to the church, which wanted all cell groups to be progressing through the same curriculum.

I can't tell you how fast the spirit of the thing dissipated. By outward appearances, our group now "fit in" better with the church. But the heart was gone. That was the end of the group for most of us.

Math clumsily attempts what art naturally accomplishes. Bruce Cockburn has a wonderful lyric that captures this:

Let's hear a laugh for the man of the world
Who thinks he can make things work
Tried to build the New Jerusalem
And ended up with New York
Ha ha ha ...[1]
                                   Selah.

WHAT MAKES
A COMMUNITY?

How do we find friends? How does one write a beautiful song or fall in love? True communities are a gift of God. One of the joys of life is discovering with whom we feel most comfortable, and with whom we do not—and that's a very unpredictable process. I liken it to when I am recording a song. I build the track instrument by instrument, all the while listening for the gaps—the places where some element is missing. As I add one element on top of another, what surprises me is that the sounds and instruments that seem most obvious to fill a certain gap often don't work at all. They sound mushy or bland in the context of the rest of the song. Rather, it is the unexpected experiment, the surprising element, that gives life to the song and takes it in an exciting new direction. It's as if music (and any other form of art) works only with a series of internal contrasts.

So it has been with many of my friendships. The people

in my life who seemed like obvious friendship material often didn't click with me, or I with them, no matter how hard we tried. But the guy who struck me as bizarre and from another planet, the one I never expected to get along with, often added something to my life that nobody else could have. The process appears random and unpredictable at times (Jesus said it would in John 3 when speaking of the Holy Spirit), but I believe the Holy Spirit is drawing us together in ways that please the Father.

Thankfully, the New Testament does show us how to carry out the relationships we find ourselves in. It also shows us some key characteristics or stages that seem to describe most human communities. I have found these stages confirmed in my own life, in my reading of history, and in the Bible. As we look at these stages of friendship—authentic love, common purpose and amazing creativity, financial generosity, rivalry, change, and reconciliation—we may discover ways to make our own friendships look more like what they were created to be.

Authentic Love

The early church was known for its love. These people were not somber-faced Christians who had been attending church together for generations while wishing they could be at the golf course or the spa instead. No, they liked each other. They thought, rightly, that they had been called to help change the world together. Paul wrote movingly at the end of many of his letters, "Greet so-and-so for me, my dear friend in the gospel." This wasn't just Middle Eastern manners; this was true relationship. We can feel the yearning and energy in his words. To me, Paul's request that Timothy bring him his cloak and books—and to "do your utmost to come before winter"—has always been especially poignant (2 Timothy 4:21).

Many artists throughout history have had strong friendships with one another similar to the kind of friendships we see in the New Testament. For example, the Impressionist painters, before they were well known or able to make a living at painting, were close friends and part of the same tightly knit social group. Renoir, Monet, Degas, and Manet would meet at a café near Manet's studio to socialize, argue, and debate. Monet said of these gatherings, "Nothing could have been more interesting than these causeries with their perpetual clash of opinions. They kept our wits sharpened.... From them we emerged with a firmer will, with our thoughts clearer and more distinct."[2]

C. S. Lewis described his writing group, the Inklings, this way:

> We meet on Friday evenings in my rooms; theoretically to talk about literature, but in fact nearly always to talk about something better. What I owe to them

is incalculable. Dyson and Tolkien were the immediate human causes of my conversion. Is any pleasure on earth as great as a circle of Christian friends by a good fire?[3]

On the other hand, Paul Gauguin wrote in a letter to his wife, "You complain about being alone. What about me? I'm alone in a room of an inn from morning till night. I have absolute silence. Nobody to exchange ideas with."[4]

Each of us longs to find the community to which we belong and to which God is calling us for the sake of his art.

Common Purpose and Amazing Creativity

It isn't often we can simply *will* a friendship into existence. Instead, relationships often form around a shared task, and there are always surprises involved. In the New Testament, unlikely candidates for friendship were bound together by a common goal—to make the gospel known—and the results changed the world. This illustrates a natural product of true friendship: a God-ordained community will live creatively.

The art movement known as Cubism emerged from the time when Picasso and Georges Braque worked together "as if roped together on a mountain."[5] Braque was Picasso's friend and artistic collaborator as they explored ideas and defined their styles. "Almost every evening, either I went to Braque's studio or Braque came to mine," Picasso later recalled. "Each of us *had* to see what the other had done during the day." Their paintings of the time were done of the same subjects and virtually in concert. Braque later recalled, "Picasso and I said things to each other that will never be said again ... that no one will ever be able to understand."[6]

Impressionism was born in a similar way. Claude Monet and Pierre-Auguste Renoir were close friends and colleagues, and in 1869, they began painting together at the river Seine. They painted boat scenes, boat parties, people taking walks along the river. They made discoveries together about light and shadow and began changing their painting styles to experiment with new techniques. Their work at the time was indistinguishable from each other's, and it was this partnership that birthed Impressionism.[7]

This is how community naturally works. We come together because of a common goal, and our work soars as a result of our authentic friendships. The Inklings— the writing group that included Tolkien, Lewis, and Charles Williams—met in a pub in Oxford, but not for the ambience. I was recently at The Eagle and Child in the very room where they met. To my surprise the room is cramped and uninspiring. I had pictured these great English academics sitting in deep leather chairs around a roaring fire, holding their pints of bitters, with room to stretch out their legs or even to pace while reading new chapters aloud from their latest books.

In reality, the long benches and chairs were wooden and hard. The walls were bare, the décor absent or uninteresting. They did not meet here for the comfort, but for the community. Tolkien later wrote, "But for the encouragement of C. S. L. I do not think that I should ever have completed or offered for publication *The Lord of the Rings.*"[8]

I have had similar, though less historically significant, experiences. For five years I traveled America and the world with Rich Wilkerson, a gifted speaker. Our friendship grew as we labored side by side, week after week. He stood by me when I faced trying circumstances. We talked at great length about our faith and struggles, and these conversations sharpened our thinking. Many of the things he said ended up in my songs, and I believe some things I told him showed up in his sermons and books. The artistic synergy was both stimulating and gratifying. Our friendship is strong to this day.

Financial Generosity

Friends are also naturally generous. They begin to hold things in common even without being directed to do so. The early church was like this. Luke wrote that the believers in Jerusalem had everything in common (Acts 2:44–45). There was financial support (1 Corinthians

16:3; Philippians 4:14–16). Paul was always arranging for certain churches to share what they had (2 Corinthians 9:1–5).

In the late 1970s, Cindy and I, along with her brother, Jeff Shively, and Bill and Beni Johnson, were part of a music group called Wild Olive. We lived in Redding, California, and traveled to all the little mountain towns in the area to sing. Late one night after a concert, we left my guitar behind, and it was never found.

I was too poor to buy a replacement. Perhaps God was sending me a message: "Get this foolish idea of traveling and singing out of your head! Stay at Bethel Church and just be happy to be the worship leader."

A few months later, in the midst of my despair, friends from Texas—Jim and Carla Miller—asked if they could stay with us. Jim piloted his own plane into Redding's airport and drove over to our house. He walked in, laid a guitar case on the floor, and opened it.

"Hey, look what the Lord did," he said.

In the case was a 1972 Martin D-28 guitar, beautiful and expensive. I knew he had been talking about buying one, so I told him how lovely it was.

"Play it," he said. So I did. Ah, what a sound!

"Jim, this is really nice!" I said.

"Well, it's yours," he replied.

"What?!" I said.

"I flew to Nashville, Chicago, Los Angeles, and San

Francisco looking for a guitar for you," he said, "and I finally found this one. It's yours. Free. No charge."

I was overwhelmed with his timely generosity. He may not have known it, but this was a critical moment that gave me the courage to continue to pursue ministry as a musician. It wasn't too long after this that I composed "Lord, Be Glorified" on that guitar. The guitar now hangs in my studio and is a constant reminder of the kindness of my friends and the goodness of God.

These sorts of acts only take on meaning in authentic communities. We should never miss the opportunity to be generous. Galatians 6:10 (NIV) reads, "Therefore, as we have opportunity, let us do good to all people, especially to those who belong to the family of believers."

Rivalry

Community almost always includes rivalry. There was rivalry among the disciples, and later among the followers of Paul and the followers of Apollos and the followers of Peter. If they had been rock stars, this would have been a battle of the bands, each lead guitarist trying to top the last one and set the bar a little higher.

Cindy and I hosted a little alfresco dinner party on a fine California summer evening a few years ago with Phil Keaggy, Lincoln and Laura Brewster, and some other musicians. Over the meal they filled the night air with stories, each getting bigger and richer. One told a story about teaching Ringo Starr the chords to his own song after they had danced the conga all night; another told about jamming with Paul McCartney in Italy. Lincoln told about going backstage at a Barbra Streisand concert in Los Angeles with his bandleader, former Journey vocalist Steve Perry. It was great fun to listen as each tried to outdo the other. We laughed a lot that evening. It was fun, yes, but still "iron sharpening iron" in the spirit of friendly rivalry.

I find it gratifying to read about great rivalries in the world of art as well, because it tells me that even the best painters and writers and sculptors were not exempt from the lesser passions. One of my favorite examples is Leonardo da Vinci and Michelangelo, who were fierce rivals and polar opposites. Da Vinci was good-looking and graceful. He first came to prominence as a musician, of all things. People liked hearing him play the lyre; he was pleasant to look at and listen to. He was socially adept and was essentially the celebrity of his day. Michelangelo, on the other hand, was comparatively graceless. His appearance was rough. He had small eyes and a flat nose. He had no social skills to speak of. He was suspicious, sensitive, quick-tempered, sarcastic, and blunt. He didn't particularly enjoy being with other people. While da Vinci went about making admirers, Michelangelo went about making enemies, when he emerged from his artist's studio at all. He took no pleasure in eating or other delights, but only in his work. He ate only because it was necessary, munching on bread while sculpting. He slept only when he had to and generally went to bed fully clothed and wearing his boots. He swung wildly between boundless optimism and inconsolable depression.[9]

Small wonder, then, that Michelangelo considered da Vinci not just his rival but his enemy. He resented and envied him. And yet the rivalry pushed both men to greater work. One time, both men were commissioned to paint murals depicting heroic scenes from Florence's history to decorate separate portions of the Grand Council's hall in the Palazzo della Signoria. Michelangelo had never liked painting very much—"painting is not my trade," he once told the pope. He preferred working in stone. But he wanted to challenge Leonardo on Leonardo's own turf. The result was one of the great artistic wonders of the day.

Da Vinci, in his usual way, set about to paint his portion of the wall early and methodically, taking more than a year to plot it out and finish it. Michelangelo characteristically started eight months later but attacked the project with such fury that he drove himself to exhaustion. His pace was far quicker than Leonardo's. People in Florence began rooting for their favorite artist the way we root for our favorite sports teams. The great competition was on.

For a time, artists came from all over to view the works

in progress, including Raphael and Cellini, who wrote in his autobiography that "while they [the murals] remained intact, they served as a school for all the world."[10]

But the wall was never finished and later was actually destroyed. Leonardo, as was his custom, had experimented with his materials to get them to stick to the wall. But the colors changed over time, and some even melted and ran down the surface. He abandoned the work.

Michelangelo was called away by a new pope to pursue projects in Rome, also leaving his portion unfinished. The murals did not survive the passage of time. So modern eyes have never seen the results of this great competition. But both men pushed each other to higher heights and in the process trained a new generation of artists through their example.[11]

Da Vinci would write in his journal, perhaps alluding to the experience:

> I say and insist that drawing in company is much better than alone, for many reasons. The first is that you would be ashamed of being seen among a number of draughtsmen if you are weak, and this feeling of shame will lead you to good study; secondly, a wholesome envy will stimulate you to join the number of those who are more praised than you are, for the praise of others will spur you on; yet another is that you can learn from the drawings of those who do better than

yourself; and if you are better than the others, you can profit by your contempt for their defects and the praise of others will incite you to further efforts.[12]

Lewis and Tolkien were rivals in addition to being friends. Tolkien often worried that Lewis was subconsciously borrowing ideas from Tolkien's then-unpublished *Lord of the Rings* and using them in his own fantasy book series, The Chronicles of Narnia. Tolkien's manner toward his friend was at times dismissive and snide: "I have just received a copy of C. S. L.'s latest: *Studies in Words*. Alas! His ponderous silliness is becoming a fixed manner," he wrote in one letter. "I am deeply relieved to find I am not mentioned."[13]

Rivalry is a spur. The disciples were rivals before Jesus' death and resurrection, and it seems to me that the spirit of healthy competition continued throughout their lives. One only has to think of Paul's discourse in which he concludes, "But I do not think I am in the least inferior to those 'super-apostles.' I may not be a trained speaker, but I do have knowledge" (2 Corinthians 11:5–6 NIV). Or his conclusion that he did not want to build on the work of any another person (Romans 15:20). Unhealthy competition? Maybe so; but I think it's more likely that we are meant to see the example of what others are doing so we pursue our own work with the greatest energy and excellence.

Change

Most of us don't plan for our relationships to end—why should something so creative, nurturing, and wonderful ever stop? Yet many relationships, even the best ones, run their course before the end of our lives. Perhaps external forces separate friends, as happened with David and Jonathan in the Old Testament. Perhaps internal forces—strong personalities, different visions for the future, and so on—cause two friends to move apart, as happened with Paul and Barnabas. Other times, friendships end by mutual consent—but still they end.

We shouldn't be surprised by this. Every story has an ending, and one song cannot go on forever. Relationships, like life, are dynamic and changing. When we try to preserve a community (or a friendship, a church, or a ministry) beyond its appointed time, it becomes a man-made thing, no longer authentic or creative.

Vincent van Gogh and Paul Gauguin painted and lived together in the fall and winter of 1888 in Provence. Their goal was to save money and create an idealistic artists' community.[14]

But the two painters argued constantly, and at times Vincent even became violent. One evening near Christmas, he got so angry that he threw a glass at Gauguin in a café. After another argument he brandished a razor at him. Vincent even cut off part of his own earlobe to spite his friend. Thus one of the most famous episodes in art history was the result of a friendship falling apart.[15]

C. S. Lewis and J. R. R. Tolkien, whose writings have had such an impact on my life and the lives of many others, had a falling out that brought their friendship to a close. "Yes, C. S. L. was my closest friend from about 1927 to 1940, and remained very dear to me," Tolkien wrote. "But in fact we saw less and less of one another after he came under the dominant influence of Charles Williams, and still less after his very strange marriage."[16]

In 1879, just ten years after he invented Impressionism with Pierre-Auguste Renoir, Claude Monet said of his Impressionist friends, "I very rarely see the men and women who are my colleagues. The little church has become a banal school which opens its doors to the first dauber." Disputes, success, war, and poverty had driven the group apart. Renoir actually abandoned Impressionism for other styles of painting.[17]

Sometimes we even lose our community through death. Leonardo da Vinci and Raphael died within a year of each other, leaving Michelangelo as the lone towering figure in European art for the next forty-five years of his life.[18]

Reconciliation

When we surf the natural ebb and flow of relationships as gracefully as we can, we usually discover that God is bringing us into exactly the community that we need in *this* season rather than what we needed in the past. And at some point, those old relationships may even be restored or recalibrated.

After Vincent van Gogh cut off his ear in a fit of anger at Paul Gauguin, the two continued to exchange personal letters and kind words until Vincent's death. The relationship found a new expression even after what appeared to be a debacle.

Tolkien and Lewis never completely abandoned each other either. Tolkien was able to write, "But we owed each a great debt to the other, and that tie with the deep affection that it begot, remains."[19]

TIPS FOR
HAVING COMMUNITY

Based on the above observations, here are a few recommendations for having successful relationships:

Enjoy true friends. They are gifts from God. Paul seemed to treasure all the friends he made during his missionary journeys. He wrote "I am glad about the coming of Stephanas, Fortunatus, and Achaicus, ... for they refreshed my spirit" (1 Corinthians 16:17–18). He called Tychicus a beloved brother (Ephesians 6:21), called Luke the beloved physician (Colossians 4:14), and began nearly

every letter with an expression of thanks for his friends and fellow Christians.

Don't let rivalry get you down. Rivalry can spur you to great heights. It is possible that God has put you in a community for this very purpose. Perhaps what you perceive as rivalry is God directing and guiding you in a new direction. If you find yourself in unwanted competition with someone in your circle of friends, just picture yourself like Lennon and McCartney, or like jazz musicians trading solos. Let it spur you on, and let it refine God's artistry in you.

Go for it with gusto. Real communities are highly productive and creative. When you find yourself in one, don't take it for granted. Throw yourself into the task, just like an artist gives himself entirely to his present work. Be like Michelangelo: sleep in your boots.

Help one another. Communities give us great opportunities to live like the early Christians did, by sharing and giving and meeting needs. One time when Rich Wilkerson and I were on the road for a week in Texas, Cindy called to tell me about a letter from the IRS that we took to mean they were levying a lien against us for many thousands of dollars. We had no idea why. When I told Rich, he immediately offered everything he had if I needed it. Thankfully, it was a mistake on the part of

the IRS, but it served to show me what a loyal friend I
had in Rich.

Recognize that communities are diverse. Being where
you belong doesn't mean everyone will be like you. The
early church was diverse—some were rich, some poor,
some Jewish, some Gentile. Even Paul's assignment as
the apostle to the Gentiles shows that shared purpose
and passion can trump shared genealogy or ethnicity.
So don't be surprised if the community God calls you to
doesn't fit your exact demographic.

Cindy and I had the great privilege of doing a tour
of the Southeast with Danniebelle Hall, one of gospel
music's true queens. We were sometimes the only white
people in the auditorium, yet it was never awkward. We
all loved Jesus, and, boy, did we have church!

Don't get hung up on who's in charge. A pastor recently
told me about meeting with several other pastors in his
city to combine their Christian schools into one. During
the discussion, the pastor of the largest church said, "You
know, someone has to be the big dog in this situation, and
I'm more than happy to be it." My friend told me this guy
always had to be the head of everything. He could only
ever be the big dog.

Saint Francis, on the other hand, who founded the
brotherly order bearing his name, willingly gave up the
leadership of the Franciscans to another priest rather than

protect his position in what could have been a protracted struggle. He did not "cling to his prerogatives" (Philippians 2:6 Phillips) but made himself a servant. History records the name of that other priest only in the reflected light of Saint Francis.

I have noticed, and maybe you have too, that some in ministry today get caught up in their role or spiritual office in the church. I have seen people call themselves Apostle So-and-So, or First Lady So-and-So, or Prophet Such-and-Such while seeming to esteem the title more than the undertaking. But as far as I can tell, the offices of the church are not titles but job descriptions. They are not meant to confer a higher hierarchical placement in the family of God, but to outline the duties given to that person. This seems to be more in line with the character of God.

Hierarchical leadership is always a struggle for position, a comparison of strengths, and a judgment of the importance of people in relation to each other. It's an equation, in other words. John Wesley said that ambition was the greatest detriment to the moving of God. Remember that the Master of all is also the Servant of all.

Be strong alone. Communities only work when each individual has a strong connection not just to each other but to God. As important as the community of believers is, Jesus did not first and foremost call us to a community, but to himself. Our relationship with God must be grounded in a private, intimate, and personal experience of him. No one can stand or answer for us before God. No one can take our place on the Potter's wheel. There are no surrogate Christians. Belonging to a vibrant community of Christians is no substitute for the strengthening, life-changing, and joy-giving experience we are privileged to be invited to have with Jesus one-on-one.

This is true of any artwork. Every word and each note of a song I write get my careful attention. Painters consider every color choice and brushstroke individually. If the church is a mosaic, each piece is created and perfected alone as well as in the greater art. So it is with you. God does not want to meet you only in the community of faith. He wants to be with you alone, to throw you on the wheel, to pull and shape the clay of your life and form you first, and primarily, in the solitude of prayer. True fellowship with others will only achieve its God-given richness when it is rooted in our practice of silence and solitude with God.

Recognize that communities come and go with time. You may grieve the passing of a set of friendships, but don't get stuck there. Paul had Wings after the Beatles. John wrote some of his best songs as a solo artist. Tolkien finished *The Lord of the Rings* after becoming estranged from Lewis. God will move us from community to community. If you do it right, you won't lose friends as you move on to the next set of relationships.

Value those old relationships. There will probably come a time when you revisit those old friends. Old rivals often become fast friends later in life. Perhaps reaffirming these old relationships is God's way of reminding us that we all belong to an eternal community and that ultimately we will be together when his artwork in us is ready for display.

4

THE ART
OF THE SPIRITUAL
DISCIPLINES

It is one thing to praise discipline,
and another to submit to it.
Miguel De Cervantes

Do we not find freedom along the
guiding lines of discipline?
**Yehudi Menuhin, American violinist
and conductor**

Discipline is not a restriction
but an aid to freedom.
Wayne Thiebaud, American pop artist

One of the wrong conclusions it might be possible to take from this book is this: living "artfully" means having a loosey-goosey approach to life, including the spiritual life. There is nothing undisciplined about real art or artists. A lazy artist is a lazy artist, just as a lazy athlete is a lazy athlete and a lazy entrepreneur is a lazy entrepreneur. Any real artist (or athlete or entrepreneur) would laugh at the idea that their craft could succeed without discipline.

Jim Miller, the Christian singer who gave me the Martin guitar and took me under his wing for a while, was a great example to me when I was young and green as a musician. It was a great honor when, early in my life as a musician, he asked if he could record one of my songs, "Skipping on the Mountains." I felt I had arrived as a real songwriter. Jim even invited me to play guitar on the song when he recorded it in southern California. No greater professional honor had been bestowed on me to that point.

Before long, I found myself in an actual recording studio for the first time. The producer ushered me into a room on the side of the glass opposite the control room. It was empty but for a microphone and a chair with a pair of headphones laying on it. He sat me down and explained that I would be hearing the rest of the instruments and vocals in my headphones, along with a "click track"— a metronome that served to keep all the musicians in rhythm. I had never played to a metronome before—and it soon showed. My guitar playing was all over the map. The click track was this slippery creature, impossible to pin down for very long, always seeming to move faster or slower than the beat in my head. The whole session went very poorly. I just couldn't reconcile the timing in my mind with the click track I was hearing. Jim and the producer were kind about it, but they eventually replaced my parts.

I came home from that experience humbled and determined to work on my timing. I began practicing with a metronome, sometimes for hours. I listened to the rough mixes of Jim's album, and the shame of my sloppy playing drove me to practice even more. While my family was gathered in the living room, I would sit alone in my little studio/office, playing and replaying the same song until I could get the timing right. Sometimes I stayed up nearly to dawn, headphones on, quietly playing the guitar to a recorded click track.

It was not easy, and perfecting it didn't come as an instantaneous gift from God or an answer to prayer. It was hard and lonely work. It took years for me to feel competent. But during a recording session one day, I noticed something strange and wonderful: the better my timing, the less I heard the click track. When I played perfectly in rhythm, the click disappeared under my own note. In fact, I got to where I could play an entire song and only hear the countdown click at the beginning of the track. This may not seem like a big deal, but for a young musician it was great to see some real progress. The closer I got to the perfection of my craft the less restrictive and controlling the click became. Rather than missing beats, and feeling rebuked by the click every time I did, I was now unaware of the click. Even though it was still there, I was dancing on top of it. I even learned to "swing," which is the term musicians use for playing artfully around the rhythm rather than simply playing on top of it. The click became something like a dance partner, and I was the lead in our pair. I had mastered the click because it had first mastered me.

Spiritual disciplines are a lot like that click track. It takes effort and discipline to develop skills that eventually become a joy. It is easy to chafe at the restrictions of the spiritual disciplines. Some people even feel that they can live without them. To me these "liberated Christians" are like the young guys playing wild guitar solos in the music stores. They sound great alone because they're playing along with the band in their own minds, but they can't play worth a dime with a real band or in the recording studio because they have no timing. To play well takes discipline. It is the disciplined dancer who is graceful, the disciplined painter who is masterful, the disciplined musician who moves us to tears. So God uses the spiritual disciplines to master us until we master them. Eventually the disciplines seem to disappear, even though they are built into the structure of our lives.

One of the most brilliant guitarists in the world told me that he doesn't even have to think about what he plays anymore. "If I can imagine it, I can do it. It just comes out of my fingers," he said. But he got there through years of grueling and boring practice—scales, intervals, and chord inversions, over and over again. Author Malcolm Gladwell writes in his book *Outliers* that the key to expert proficiency in any endeavor is ten thousand hours of practice[1]—and the calluses on this guitarist's fingers testify to that price.

As free as we are in Christ, the spiritual life still takes discipline—a lot of discipline. One friend of mine, looking at an early draft of this book, thought I was being too demanding in parts and suggested I tone it down. But, as I told him, God is more exacting than any legalist. We would not expect anything else from a great Artist. He aims for perfection in everything he does. At the same time, he is the God of all grace, loving his enemies and covering our sins.

Grace does not suspend the need for discipline or negate the rule of sowing and reaping. If you were looking for a free pass out of mastering the spiritual disciplines, you won't receive it here. As an artist and a fellow believer, I can tell you that art and the Christian walk take a tremendous amount of discipline. The good news is that the purpose of discipline is mastery, and mastery is what allows us to become liberated—and to become great art. Let's see how this works at an everyday level with some of the most important and essential disciplines.

TITHING

Tithing is math, but generosity is art. Yet we learn through tithing to live artfully in generosity. Remember, math serves art.

God called the Israelites to tithe the firstfruits of their labors. (What an artful and wise idea! Rather than a fixed amount, they gave in proportion to their own profit.) Though Christians may or may not be required by the new covenant to tithe (please have that debate with someone near you, not with me), the discipline of giving can and must, through practice, become a habit of generosity. We learn generosity by being mastered by a discipline of regular giving.

The truth is, God doesn't want 10 percent of what you have—he wants it all! He doesn't call you only to carefully divide the mint, anise, and cumin, like the Pharisees did in Jesus' time; he calls you to give everything you are and have to him. If we keep to a strict count of our contributions, we are no better than the servant who feared his master and buried his investment money. The artful life is lived in generosity and sacrifice.

Some people debate for years whether or not they should tithe, and to whom, and if they should tithe on their net or their gross income, and at the end of the month or immediately after receiving a paycheck. These questions are often symptomatic of someone who has not yet learned generosity. True generosity sweeps such questions away with a big, magnanimous arm. When called to give, we shouldn't start counting the pennies. Generosity rounds up. It goes overboard, just like God does.

One of the most generous people I've ever known is a pastor in Michigan who seems to always be giving. When I visit his church, the offerings are always generous. When we go out to eat, he gives crazy-big tips to the server. When he starts feeling tight with his money, he immediately writes a check for a thousand dollars to some ministry just to get rid of any creeping stinginess. This man has moved from the discipline of giving to the joy of giving—and he is a joy to be around! His attitude is infectious, and it should come as no surprise that his large church is one of the best places to worship that I have ever visited.

When I think of over-the-top generosity, my mind often goes to the transforming incident in Victor Hugo's

Les Misérables. The priest gives the silver candlesticks to Valjean after Valjean has stolen the rest of the set. It was so absurd and unaccountable that it broke Valjean's paradigm and enabled him to live outside of the math mentality and move into art.

God always intended generosity to be art, not math. Recall this admonition from the Old Testament: "Tell the Israelites to bring me an offering. You are to receive the offering for me from each man *whose heart prompts him to give*" (Exodus 25:2 NIV, emphasis mine). God did not state a percentage and apply it to everyone. He allowed for promptings of the heart and for different responses (or no response) from every individual. Similarly, God said to Moses in Deuteronomy 15:10, "Give generously to him and do so without a grudging heart; then because of this the LORD your God will bless you in all your work and in everything you put your hand to" (NIV). God's priority is clearly the attitude of the heart. This accords perfectly with what Paul wrote in 2 Corinthians 9:7 (NIV): "Each man should give what he has decided in his heart to give, not reluctantly or under compulsion, for God loves a cheerful giver."

I was among a group of Christian musicians and speakers who traveled to Honduras to get a close-up look at the ministry of Compassion International. One day, we visited a school at lunch time and were conscripted to hand out meals. As we were running back and forth delivering food to hungry children, I paused to take in the somewhat surreal scene. Here were household names of the Christian community carrying cups of juice and plates of rice and beans, wiping snotty noses, shaking grubby hands, offering themselves as servants for these children, the poorest of the poor. After lunch we were sitting on the edge of a rickety platform in the school yard while some of the group played soccer with the kids and a few of the musicians jammed. Compassion's president, Dr. Wess Stafford, told me about a time years before on a similar trip when the singer sitting with us had given his guitar away to a little boy who showed an interest in it. That little boy grew up to be a nationally known worship leader in his country. God can do a lot with our cheerful generosity.

The only way I know to become a cheerful giver is to give until it becomes a joy. That is a type of math morphing into art.

PRAYER LISTS
AND DEVOTIONS

Prayer is an important discipline. But I'm sure most of us have gotten the feeling at times that we're workers in God's factory and that prayer is merely a matter of presenting our requisition list to Jesus, the foreman.

But what if prayer is spending relational time with

God? What if through prayer we come to know him, enjoy him, and strengthen our relationship with him? Jesus said eternal life is to know God (John 17:3). Jesus also said that when we enter a relationship with him, eternity starts right now. We pass over from death to life (John 5:24). Prayer is the practice of eternal communion with God in our temporal world.

In prayer we get to know God, and he gets to know us. The word for *know* used in John 17 is the same as when Matthew tells us that Joseph awoke from his dream and took Mary as his wife—but didn't "know" her. This "knowing" is the open, unguarded heart of God telling us he desires us to know him intimately, meet him privately, and share the secrets of love.

How do we get to know people? Talking is one way, but it may not be the best. In silence we cannot hide. Words can be used as barriers, deflectors, smoke screens. Words can cover the truth as easily as they reveal it, but silence reveals the true heart.

What is prayer, then? Jesus told the disciples how to pray, and that model prayer has been dissected in many books more ambitious than this one. I wonder if the prayer Jesus taught us is only the beginning, leading us to a deeper communion with God. Perhaps the most important aspect of prayer is simply communion— relationship, silence. This takes discipline.

Early in our marriage, Cindy and I talked through

everything. Like most young people, we felt compelled to share our feelings on everything from minor incidents to major disagreements. But over time, Cindy and I both realized something: talking can waste a lot of time and energy. These days we find ourselves sitting in silence more and more. Many "issues" we formerly would have dealt with in hours of spoken argument can be sorted out with long spans of considered silence and then a few healing comments.

It seems so easy now, but it was a hard lesson to learn, and it took great discipline at times to hold our tongues and trust the silence. That discipline has paid off in many ways, saving both of us heartache and building up our trust in each other as we more carefully weigh our words before speaking them. Proverbs says, "A fool vents all his feelings, but a wise man holds them back" (29:11).

The discipline of prayer, too, can be difficult and seem like wasted time. I have heard ministers say that we shouldn't even pray at all if we pray only out of duty. But that's like saying we should work only when we feel like it, or practice an instrument when it suits us, or talk to our spouses only when we're feeling love for them. It's a silly suggestion. The duty of prayer, like any other duty, is intended to lead us to the mastery of prayer—which is intimacy with God. The more disciplined effort we put into a relationship the stronger and richer it will be. Would my marriage to Cindy be rich and strong if all we ever did was exchange our "honey-do" lists? No way. I would miss her intelligence and humor, not to mention the warmth of her love. Yet we have had to train ourselves to embrace the full relationship in all its possibilities. I believe prayer is the same. It is the path to experiencing God in the full range of fellowship he desires. It is worth practicing with the same intensity and discipline with which a master artist works on a masterpiece.

THE RITUALS OF THE CHURCH

Many Christians hear the word *rituals*, and their eyes glaze over. They fancy themselves "free" of rituals, free to express themselves to God without bondage to legalistic rites. But abandoning rituals means abandoning a special kind of art that God uses to bind us to him and to each other.

One of the most memorable times in my spiritual life happened when Cindy and I had gone to Europe with some other Jesus People for a summer of ministry. In London we stayed at the Youth With A Mission house at 8 Vermont Road, next to an Anglican church. The young priest came to welcome us and invite us to join him for prayer early the next morning. I decided to do it, so I arose before the sun and made my way next door and into the sanctuary. It was dark at first. The sanctuary was redolent of that holy combination of candle wax, old books, and ancient stone (which brought to mind the English description of their churches as "smells and bells"). Soon the early light coming through the stained-glass clerestory windows high overhead reflected on the ornate gold altar and gave the apse a warm glow.

To my surprise I was the only one there, other than the priest.

He did not acknowledge the small size of his congregation. Rather, he bade me good morning and invited me to kneel at the altar rail. Then he handed me *The Book of Common Prayer* and said, formally and in a wonderful English accent, "Please turn to page 62. I shall read the priest parts, and you shall read the congregational response. Is that clear?" I said yes, and we proceeded to pray these distillations of the spiritual longings of the saints over many different centuries. We confessed our sins, were absolved before God, proclaimed his greatness, and took Communion together, just the two of us. Years later I wrote a song about the experience.

> *The smell of burning candles and hand-rubbed aging*
> *   wood*
> *The clamor of the large bells and the chiming of the small*
> *The signing of some secret not wholly understood*
> *The joining of the voices great and small*
> *The muffled cry of supplicants now kneeling at their post*

The measured move of wise and holy men
The ancient prayers so crafted to both wound and soothe
* the soul*
The longing at the heart of every hymn.
What's missing from my life is this ritual
The slow step of a priest on a paving stone.
What's wanting most in me is the miracle
Of meeting God in silence
And stepping out this ritual alone.

What I had done with the priest in that Anglican church was to take part in an artistic expression of our shared beliefs. You see, the rituals of the church are like little one-act plays. Each ritual tells a story about what we believe. For example, when we baptize sinners in water, we are not making some heavenly exchange or spiritual transaction—"closing the sale" with God and getting our salvation to show up on heaven's ledger. Rather, we are participating in the same small play that Jesus himself participated in and endorsed. He willingly stepped into the artwork of it that day at the Jordan River, though Jesus was sinless and had no spiritual "need" of salvation or baptism. I love the reason Jesus gave John the Baptist for doing it: "to fulfill all righteousness" (Matthew 3:15). Jesus had his eye on the bigger picture, the grand sweep of God the Father's magnificent creative vision, of which water baptism is one expression. He affirmed the goodness of God's art by his participation, which is why believers today carry out this same one-act play. The pastor plays the part of John the Baptist. The baptismal tank (or other water container) stands in for the Jordan River, and the sinner identifies himself with Jesus. Into the water we go, as into the grave, and out we come, rising into new life. It is a visual poem of the Christian story, a mystical work of art in which we identify with our Savior.

The solemn joining of a man and a woman in holy matrimony is another of these one-act plays. It is both a remembrance of the union of the first man and woman and a prophetic picture of the coming union of Christ and his bride.

Likewise, we "proclaim the Lord's death till He comes" in the Holy Communion (1 Corinthians 11:26), drinking from the cup and eating the bread. We act out the death, burial, and resurrection of Jesus and remember his sacrifice for us. Like all art, this ritual "proclaims" something—in this case the most powerful truth in the universe, the mysterious truth of the cross.

Even prayer can be a small heavenly drama. Jesus introduced what we call the Lord's Prayer by saying, "In this manner, therefore, pray" (Matthew 6:9). It's as though he handed us a script and said, "Here are your lines." Countless times I have led or participated in this prayer in a congregational setting, and almost every time something leaps out at me as though I was hearing it for the first time.

There are many other rituals we could point to, but let me bring up just one more: the ritual of confession and forgiveness. The Bible tells us to confess our sins to one another, and whoever's sins we forgive, they are forgiven. This is another of these one-act plays. We are called upon to be a confessor for our friends. Each time this happens, the confessor and the one needing forgiveness step momentarily into a sacred drama. We are being drawn into the heavenly art of forgiveness.

Most evangelical denominations have rejected the rituals of the high church. You won't find many fundamentalists genuflecting and crossing themselves. What perhaps went unnoticed in the rejection is that people will not exist in a "ritual vacuum." The soul longs for the shared art of these one-act plays. What evangelicals substitute in their place are, by and large, traditions of men—accumulations of "sacred" practices from previous generations such as a specific order of service, altar benches, altar calls, extending our hands toward someone as we pray, enthusiastic worship, hiring youth pastors, or the iconography of our modern houses of worship. Whereas the high churches have a scriptural explanation for each of their rituals, evangelicals are hard-pressed to find any theological underpinnings for theirs.

Perhaps the original evangelical complaint was valid
—that the life had gone out of the rituals and they were
being used as coercive tools in the hands of greedy, politi-
cally minded clergy. However, misuse does not preclude
proper use. Paul seems to have addressed this when he
wrote about some believers "having a form of godliness
but denying its power" (2 Timothy 3:5). It seems that he
treasured both the form *and* the power. Ritual, at its best,
includes both. Why else would Jesus have said, "Do this
in remembrance of Me" (Luke 22:19)?

In one of his supernatural thrillers Charles Williams depicts an Anglican Archdeacon throughout the
book saying to himself under his breath, "This also is
Thou; neither is this Thou."[2] He recognized the paradox
that God is in all things yet not fully expressed in any
one thing; that the form of something can be alive and
dynamic, or as dead as a statue. Such is art, and such are
the one-act plays we participate in, as believers have done
down through the millennia: "This also is Thou; neither
is this Thou."

FELLOWSHIP

Christian community will always be mysterious and surprising, but there is an aspect of discipline to maintain-
ing it as well. The writer to the Hebrews told us not to
forsake meeting together (Hebrews 10:25). As much as

we may want to skip this command at times, it still holds. However, many Christians approach church attendance as though it were just another calendar obligation, like soccer practice or an annual medical exam. When going to church becomes a duty we check off our list each week, we reduce its importance to the level of all the other obligations we undertake, and we sit firmly in the First Church of the Equation.

To find the art in fellowship we must be mastered by the discipline of committing ourselves to a group of fellow Christians. We must begin by realizing the privilege we have to gather with other believers. Given how much of the church suffers across the globe, religious freedom is no small thing to be thankful for. Then we take on the duty of showing up and being a contributing member of a local body. Yes, it can be a drudgery sometimes. But we do it even when we don't feel up to it, or when we are having difficulties with the pastor or other members, because we have committed ourselves to it. The difference between math and art in fellowship is that some never get past the duty of it, while others embrace the duty as an act of devotion, discipline, and love—and eventually find themselves with a welcome mastery in the area of relationships.

THE DANGER OF BECOMING A "PROFESSIONAL" CHRISTIAN

The trick in all of this is to avoid rote living. It is easy to start seeing ourselves as "professional" Christians who carry out the necessary rituals. For example, I have made my living advocating for the Christian life since I was seventeen. I derive my support from standing before audiences and speaking in favor of Jesus Christ. At first I didn't take up an offering. I was an amateur—that is, one who does what he does for love, not money. Even after I began to be paid for singing and ministering, I considered myself an amateur. I never spoke in terms of my "career" in music. It was a calling. I was passionate about it. I had to be—the honorariums I received were sometimes so tiny, I certainly couldn't be doing it for the money. I recall one pastor paying me for two nights of ministry by pouring six dollars worth of coins into my open palms. The first year of our ministry, our taxable income was $1,700. Someone in the California tax system found an excuse to send us a check for $800, even though we'd never paid a dime into the system.

Over the years I made more money, had more kids, bought a bigger house, hired people to work with us, got larger offices, put out better albums, paid taxes, and spent more money on just about everything. Now we were a machine that needed fuel, and the fuel was money. And then one day my wife made a comment about my career. I was taken aback. This was not a career; it was still my calling. Yet I had been doing it for a long-enough time that in everyone else's eyes it was my career.

That has bothered me ever since, and I have endeavored to never think of what I do as a career, though it has careerlike qualities. I know I have worked and practiced hard enough that I have developed some professional skills. This is dangerous because it offers me the choice to speak of Jesus merely because I have developed the ability to do it, and it pays my bills. It happens to good people, who perhaps never see it coming. It has happened to some ministers I have known. They seemed to be great examples of propriety and ministry until one day they flipped out, ran off with the organist, abandoned their families, and sold used cars or insurance for a living. One went to Las Vegas and became (no joke) an Elvis impersonator. Fitting, isn't it? He went from one act to another. I suppose he'd had some practice.

Years ago, a wise friend talked to me about fame and its dangers. He thought I was on the cusp of some fame. His counsel was that I should endeavor to ensure that the image and the reality of who I am should be the same — a unity of being. I have heeded his words. I daily fight against my own hypocrisy. I am a professional. I am not a professional Christian. I am a follower of Christ. If for nothing else, I want to pursue my calling well so my children and grandchildren continue to be shaped by how I live, not repelled by some hollow ritual that I carry out in a grotesque parody of the Christian life.

This kind of "professional Christian syndrome" can afflict anyone. We can all become professional at our faith if we are not careful. We do it by embracing the disciplines and forgetting that the point of it all is mastery. We are intended to rise from math to art, not to make a show of our math-y lifestyle. That is when we become empty, legalistic. We tithe regularly but never become generous. We pray faithfully, but not for the love of being with God.

The members of U2, Christendom's unofficial house band, had a saying when they were just starting out. They would see other bands perform, and they would say to themselves, "Everything but *It*." They meant that the other band's musical style was in place—the look, the attitude, the energy, even the fans—but the band was missing some key element that made their art matter. U2 has *It*. That is what makes their music and their concerts transcendent for so many.

I meet many professing Christians, unfortunately, who have everything but *It*. I have met ministers who don't believe anymore. Some of them were my good friends. I meet churchgoing people all the time who have

asily as to him. We can develop a form of godliness
t, like a sculpture of God, looks like him but has no
wer.

Spiritual disciplines can also lead us back to God.
hese beautiful one-act plays can express the obedience
nd love we have toward him and the unity we have with
other believers. Maybe it is time for you to be mastered
again by some discipline, some spiritual skill, so that you
can one day master it—and find freedom. There will
come a time when you become graceful. The click track
will disappear, and you will dance around the beat without ever losing your timing.

no relationship with Jesus. They are n̶
like Peter, who had nowhere else to go
the words of eternal life" (John 6:68). The
something else. They love the artifice, not
love the practices of the church and the appea
Christian lifestyle, or perhaps church remin̶
good times in their past. Maybe these are the on
who will welcome them. Whatever the reason, the
Christ's church but don't know him.

If U2 were just another band and Bono just the dir
tive son of an amateur opera singer, I would have dev̶
about thirty seconds to them as I flipped through Rolli̶
Stone magazine in the early 1980s. Their music woul̶
not have spoken to me and grabbed my heart the way it
did when I first heard the song "Gloria" — "Gloria exul-
tate. Oh Lord, if I had anything, anything at all, I'd give
it to you" — from their second album, *October.* Their art,
like all real art has *It*, and *It* is a person — the Artist. God
is who we must look for in every ritual, every practice.
Without the Artist — when we have everything but *It* —
all of our endeavors are, in the end, meaningless.

As we practice the disciplines, we are faced with the
choice of loving the art more than the Artist, the image
more than the Person. Perhaps it has happened to you.
Jesus said, "Without Me you can do nothing" (John
15:5). Rituals and disciplines can lead us away from him

5

THE ART
OF SHARING
OUR FAITH

Art does not take kindly to facts,
is helpless to grapple with theories,
and is killed outright by a sermon.
Agnes Repplier, American essayist

Every artist dips his brush in his own soul,
and paints his own nature into his pictures.
**Henry Ward Beecher, nineteenth-century
pastor and abolitionist**

You can only find truth with logic if you
have already found truth without it.
G. K. Chesterton

I got to see U2 perform at the Cow Palace in San Francisco on their "Unforgettable Fire" tour. The concert was unlike any I had ever attended because it felt like the gathering of a community. As the band played a cover of Bob Dylan's "Knocking on Heaven's Door," Bono found a member of the audience who could play the guitar, brought him onto the stage, strapped his old Gibson on him—and the next thing we knew, the young guy was playing with the band! Then, one by one, the band members left the stage, and this audience member was left standing there alone, playing his part on Bono's guitar while the rest of us sang along—"Knock, knock, knockin' on heaven's door." It was an incredible moment—thrilling, dangerous, and alive. This spectator, this guy who'd bought a ticket and showed up, had literally become part of the show. He had been invited into the art. We all watched him play the guitar, and we sang along and rejoiced with him as if it were us— because it was. He was our representative up there strumming away. Through him, each member of the audience became a participant in a U2 concert.

That's what real evangelism looks like. For many Christians, "evangelism" is a chore carried out without any real emotional consequence—like we are salespeople for some Cosmic Salvation Company. But evangelism at its most basic level is an invitation into relationship and community, both with God and with other believers. One of the most attractive things about Christ is the loving, authentic community he leads. Jesus told us plainly that love would be the appealing thing about us: "By this all will know that you are My disciples, if you have love for one another" (John 13:35). That is a remarkable fact— the potency of the gospel message rests in the vibrancy of our human relationships and in the attractiveness of our community.

When evangelism offers a salvation equation—a math-based promise—it misses the whole point. My experience teaches me that people meet Christ in the context of relationships far more often than by reading the Four Spiritual Laws in a tract. This is exactly what Jesus predicted would happen. He gave us the secret to evangelism —"Love one another"—only to see us ignore it time after time. Love is replaced by proselytizing, and evangelistic events masquerade as true community. But unbelievers are not usually waiting around to be convinced by some final step of doctrinal logic; they are waiting for the right community to come along. Show them a truly loving group of people, and they won't care how it works—they will just want to belong.

I saw this play out one summer when I was part of

a group of young people who went to the University of California at Berkeley to share our faith. We went out street-witnessing every day. For the uninitiated, that means we went out into public places pamphleteering for the gospel and trying to talk about Jesus with whomever would spend a few moments in conversation with us. The stretch of Telegraph Avenue that ended at the university's Sproul Plaza was, at that time, a tie-dyed, patchouli parade of freaks and misfits—students and professors, hippies, activists, druggies, homeless teenagers, and dirty con men. It was like being in a noisy Third World country. There were drum circles, street musicians, and panhandlers, all trying to crank up the volume level. Jesus was popular at this time and had become a catchphrase for that generation, so it was easy at first to talk about him to these searching souls. But when they found out we were Christians, most people snapped shut and wouldn't listen to our message. They weren't willing to accept that Jesus was the Lord of the universe; they wanted him to remain just another bright star in their constellation of gods.

After a few days of this, one afternoon five us headed to the Laundromat on Telegraph Avenue a few blocks from the campus to wash some clothes (yes, Jesus People washed their clothes). We were sitting in a circle on the floor, laughing and singing songs together as we waited for our clothes to tumble dry. One member of our group tacked on the bulletin board a poster for our end-of-the-week evangelistic meeting. Nearby was a fellow also doing his wash who was eavesdropping on our group. He was a genuine long-haired, bearded, trippin' hippie freak in his midthirties. We didn't know it at the time, but he was involved in some pretty destructive behavior. We never spoke to him. After all, we weren't there to witness, but to do laundry. But after we left, he took the poster off the bulletin board, wondering who we were and what we were all about. Something about us intrigued him. That Friday he came to our meeting and met Jesus. He was radically transformed—forgiven, cleansed, and set on a new path of life. As far as I know, he was the only lasting fruit from that entire week of ministry. And it didn't happen because we "witnessed" to him, but because he saw the community of faith alive in that Laundromat. He joined our group and went on to be involved in ministry in the Bay Area.

There is a collision between what many people think will work—pamphleteering, proselytizing, "witnessing" —and what actually introduces people to Jesus. We have taken the art of evangelism and turned it into a series of equations—a ministry of math. In the process we have removed the one thing that makes us so attractive— loving relationships with God and one another. We have substituted a proper belief system, and yet the essential eternal issue between God and us is not whether we know the truths of Christianity but whether we know God. Relationships are of primary importance. Can we expect a God who places such emphasis on knowing him to allow us to skip knowing other people in favor of simply peppering them with a gospel "message"?

Let me run through some of the inartistic ideas and habits that have crept into our understanding of evangelism. The sooner we see how math has infiltrated our efforts the sooner we can let God's art take over again.

JESUS NEVER TOLD US TO WIN ANYONE

As I mentioned before, there is only one reference in the New Testament to someone being "won"—1 Peter 3:1, where wives are told that their husbands can be won "without a word." Jesus *did* call us to tell the story and make disciples—which is not to be confused with making converts. There seems to be a crucial middle step missing in his command—the moment of conversion, which is that step after hearing and before becoming a disciple. In our version of evangelism, we often focus on an isolated, individual moment—the point at which the sinner "prays the sinner's prayer" and "accepts Jesus Christ as his personal Lord and Savior." But is it possible that Jesus was leaving us out of that part of conversion intentionally? Is it possible that we have taken a burden on our shoulders that was not meant for us?

It seems to me that we have inserted ourselves into the mystical work of salvation that belongs to the Holy Spirit. We have come to believe that we are indispensable to the process, that the salvation of the world depends on us. We fixate on the moment of conversion, even though the Bible doesn't. One wise friend reminds me that if we can claim any power to win people to Jesus, it is at the expense of the cross. "And I, if I am lifted up from the earth, will draw all peoples to Myself," Jesus said (John 12:32).

When my wife's brother, Jeff, was eighteen, he was living in Indiana and working a high-paying factory job. He was very handsome and fashionable, had his own apartment, and drove a little red sports car. Girls fell all over him. He seemed to have everything he wanted.

Jeff came out to California to spend Christmas with our family, and one night we got into a wide-ranging discussion about the antichrist, the Kennedy assassination, the end times, and other spiritual issues. Cindy and I let the conversation begin and end naturally, without manipulating it to be "evangelistic." A few days later he headed back to Indiana.

Five months later, we received a letter from Jeff that

told us about his deep dissatisfaction with his life and his desire to have peace. "When I saw you at Christmas, I could tell you had something. Whatever you guys have, I want it" is the way he put it. We wrote him back to say that all we had was Jesus. About a month later, we drove cross-country and stopped in Indiana to visit relatives. Jeff told us that when he had received our letter he gave himself to Jesus. He packed up his little red sports car with all his belongings and followed us out to California to live with us and grow in his newfound faith.

I don't know that we can claim to have "led Jeff to the Lord," though that's what he told people. Rather, we did what felt comfortable and natural. We were being ourselves, not doing a job or giving a sales pitch. *God* was the one wooing Jeff to himself, and he called to him in a much deeper way than we ever could have. Some might criticize us for not "closing the sale" with Jeff during that conversation or before he left to go back home. But Jesus himself missed a great opportunity to close the sale in Mark 12. When a scribe answered him well, Jesus merely said, "You are not far from the kingdom of God" (verse 34). Many ministers today would have asked for every head to be bowed and every eye to be closed and had the fellow raise his hand or come to the front for prayer. Jesus simply affirmed that God was coming very close to that scribe. How un-mathlike!

I have kept a running count in my mind of all the churches I have been in or read about that proudly published their evangelistic gains. According to my unofficial tally, everybody in America has been saved, some more than once. I've been in churches of five hundred that had five thousand "salvations" in the last year. I looked around their auditorium and asked myself, "Well, where are they?" They were counting conversions, not disciples. Big difference.

At this point you might lump me in with those Christians who reject, and sometimes mock, the good work done by many evangelists over the centuries. I am not one of those. I believe in the calling of the evangelist. You would rightly say that I have spent my life being a musical evangelist—though most people don't call it evangelism when you have a guitar hanging around your neck. My wife was touched by God at a Billy Graham crusade in Tucson, Arizona, when she was twelve years old, and it made a lasting difference in her life. Concentration camp survivor Corrie ten Boom laid hands on Cindy's stomach and prayed for our unborn first child. I thank God for anyone who is willing to stand in public and risk ridicule to tell God's story.

But I believe evangelism is much more than that. It is a form of art that is relational, creative, and patient—a form of art to which all Christians are called.

OUR TRADITIONAL SALVATION PHRASES ARE FOREIGN TO THE BIBLE

We evangelicals have developed a set of salvation-related phrases that aren't in the Bible, and yet we believe strongly enough about them that we look sideways at anyone who doubts them. I'm sure you've heard of "praying the sinner's prayer" and "accepting Jesus Christ into your heart" and talking about Jesus as your "personal Lord and Savior"—but these phrases are not found in the New Testament. I'm not suggesting that they are untrue or that at one time they didn't communicate something important. I am saying that we have allowed them to form a doctrine of their own about who God is and how we become his—and it has spread like kudzu over all the other doctrines in our theological landscape.

For example, as I mentioned earlier, most Christians fixate on the "moment of salvation," as though there was a way to pin down the precise instant when we click over from sinner to saint. Testimonies offered at churches or small groups hinge on this moment, and people who don't have a precise moment of salvation often feel inferior to those who do. If we believe in a math God, then salvation is a binary choice—zero or one, on or off—and it's easy to pin down a specific time—you just look back in the logbook. But many, perhaps most, people who come to believe in Jesus know that it was more than a moment. It was a process, a gestation, a push through the birth canal, a dance, a struggle, a wrestling match—an often indefinable movement toward God.

When asked how her new book was coming along, one well-known author replied that it was finished; she had only to write it down. C. S. Lewis famously said that he got on an hourlong bus ride as a heathen and got off it as a Christian. When did that author write her book? When did Lewis become a believer? When does a painter begin his painting? Is it when he first conceives of an idea for a piece of art, or buys the canvas, or puts it on the easel, or applies the first dab of paint, or signs it? Is this question even relevant to the artist?

I've already referred to Paul's words in Romans 8:29, "for whom He foreknew, He also predestined to be conformed to the image of His Son," Jesus Christ. These words *foreknew* and *predestined* tell us that God had the idea of you before you were born. God had already envisioned the artwork you could be and, like the famous author above, only needed to work it out in your life. That vision for your life is much more important than placing undue importance on an often artificial or arbitrary moment of conversion.

PEOPLE ALREADY KNOW
THEY ARE SINNERS

One of the great myths of evangelism is that people don't know they are sinners. I have never met a single person who did not already know that he or she was a sinner. They may not have phrased it that way. They might have said, "Nobody's perfect," or, "Well, of course, I haven't done everything right. I've made some mistakes." But what they meant was, in essence, "I have sinned and fallen short of the glory of God." What is our message to these people?

I was singing at a lunchtime concert in Union Square, San Francisco, and as I looked out over the crowd, a man caught my eye. He had maneuvered his way to the front of the stage. He carried a big sign that said something like "Turn or Burn!" or "You are going directly to hell." Because I was singing about Jesus, he appeared to be with me! To make it worse, he was wearing earphones, listening to music, and showing no interest in engaging people in dialogue or relationship. With his offensive sign he was pointing people to the unsatisfactory equation of their lives—and hoping this would somehow make the gospel attractive.

I couldn't let the perceived association stand. I stopped my song abruptly midway through, pointed him out, and said, "He's not with me. I didn't come to tell you

you're going to hell. I came to tell you how you can go to heaven." He saw me point him out, smiled, and gave me a thumbs-up because he thought I was affirming him. He couldn't even hear what I was saying! He may have gone home that day and patted himself on the back because he had "shared the gospel," but had he really? I can't think of a less artistic way to do it.

People get that they are sinners. They don't need to be told again. They need to see in your life and mine the heavenly relationship that will draw them like lost children back into the family of God.

LET GOD DISPLAY YOU

So what *has* God called us to do? What part do we play in bringing people to faith? Evangelism is mostly about *being* and *being together*. Being who we are allows God to show off his artworks in progress—us; being together with other believers shows the loving community that attracts people.

Artwork always reveals the artist. Nobody looks at a Monet and confuses it for a Warhol. Or points to a Renoir and says, "Michelangelo really hit his stride when he was painting those boat parties." We know artists by their art. Many times I have heard a song and known who wrote it before reading the credits because I recognized their unmistakable style. When an artist is creating his true art, there is no way he can hide himself. What and how he paints or writes or composes shows us the kind of person he is. Every artist is intimately present in his art. Since we are God's art, he will make himself known through us when we surrender to him fully and allow him the freedom to express himself. People will know the kind of person God is by your actions more than your words. Remeber Irenaeus's words: "The glory of God is man fully alive."[1]

A woman approached me recently after I had spoken about this subject and said, "I understand what you're saying about God. I knew my dad through his art. He was a painter and a poet and a very quiet man. I would stand by his side as he painted, and sometimes he would look at me and say, 'Watch this,' then fling some paint spectacularly across the canvas, and we both would laugh. I knew him and I loved him through his art."

Our job is to let God display us when and where he wills. That means we have to be ready to answer questions about what we believe as the Spirit directs us. On those occasions, we will be called to be a witness. Notice I use *witness* as a noun. Only in modern times have we Christians mistakenly turned that word into a verb. In a court of law, a witness is called to testify to what he has experienced, not what he believes. If you told the judge that, though you hadn't seen it happen, you believed that John fired the gun that killed Mary, he would have your comment stricken from the record and remind you that you are to tell only what you actually experienced. The court is not interested in what you believe. It is not even interested in your giving someone else's testimony, which is called hearsay. It is only interested in what you have seen and heard—a model exemplified by the disciples and the early church in the book of Acts.

Too many Christians, when speaking of their faith, are telling what they believe (and hope) to be true, not what they have personally experienced of God. They might even be telling someone else's story, things about Jesus they heard from others. Is it any wonder, then, that the listener recognizes the lack of authenticity and mentally strikes it from the record? John said that what he had heard, seen, and handled of the Word of God was what he spoke about (1 John 1:1–3). He didn't traffic in hearsay.

John 9 records a wonderfully candid example of a good witness in action. Jesus healed a blind man by telling him to wash in the pool of Siloam. The man's neighbors were astounded at this miracle and promptly brought him before the Pharisees, who grilled him about Jesus and how this miracle had been performed. They told him that Jesus was a sinner. The man replied that he didn't know whether he was a sinner—all he knew was that he was blind before but now he could see. I love that! It completely lacks any sort of theology or religion. He was the perfect witness—he stuck to what he had experienced. Do we?

ONE AT A TIME

When my daughter, Britt, was two years old, she and I were driving to the store together. She was very quiet, obviously in deep thought, when she suddenly said, "Dad, I know how many people there are in the world."

I said "Really, Britt. How many are there?"

She replied, "Two hundred."

Her words got me thinking, and I realized that she was just about right: there were around two hundred people in *my* world—people I knew and could directly influence for good or bad.

When we returned home, I got my calculator out and began to run some numbers. If the greatest evangelist in the world could win a thousand people to Jesus every night of the year, and he never took a vacation and none of those converts "backslid," we would, of course, pour money into his ministry. This looks like a very good return on investment. However, it would take him over 16,400 years to win the present population of the world to Jesus. That's nearly three times longer than the recorded history of the world.

On the other hand, if one person brought one other person to Jesus and spent a year walking beside that new believer, and each new believer brought another person to Jesus the next year, and so on, this cell-like growth would introduce the whole world to Jesus in just thirty-three years. Effective, yes. Realistic, perhaps. Sexy, no. It doesn't have the motivational quotient of a big event.

Yet, isn't it so much more artistic and personal (and effective) to welcome each one into the family of God individually than to lump all non-Christians together on the conveyor belt of mass-produced salvation?

BE READY FOR DISPLAY— EVEN AT ODD TIMES

Where and when we are displayed for God's glory is often not up to us. One time I was boarding an airplane bound for Alaska when the flight attendant noticed I had my guitar with me.

"You play guitar?" she said excitedly. "What's your name?"

I told her my name was Bob and was about to add that I wasn't anybody famous when she whirled around, grabbed the public address microphone, and said to all the gathered passengers waiting for the same flight, "Ladies and gentlemen, we have entertainment on our flight tonight! This is Bob, and he's going to be singing for us on our way to Alaska."

Everybody who was reading, sleeping, or pretending to read or sleep came alive and started clapping. Suddenly there was going to be a party.

I was shocked. I started praying for the immediate rapture of the church. Then I prayed that her idea would be forgotten and that we would have a typical, boring flight. No such luck. At the end of her safety demonstration, the flight attendant made sure to add, "and Bob will be singing for us tonight!"

I had no idea what I might do for a "concert" since this was not a church and not all of these people were Christians. But I had the distinct feeling that God was going to display me, whether I wanted it or not. Midway through the flight, I heard the flight attendant's voice in my ear: "Are you ready?"

"I guess so," I said.

She announced to everyone that it was time for a concert at the back of the plane. All but two passengers got up, went to the back, and waited for me to provide the entertainment. The flight attendant folded one seat down so I could sit facing the people. I still didn't know what songs I should play.

"I'm happy to sing for you tonight, but I may not know all the songs you want to hear," I started. "I'm a Christian singer, and—"

I was cut off by a drunk fellow, who, upon hearing the word *Christian*, let out a disgusted "humph!" and slumped back in his chair. I have enough stage experience to know when emergency measures are called for, so I launched into a popular song that was then at the top of the charts. The people jumped in and sang heartily with me. We moved on to songs by the Beatles, Crowded House, U2, and the Police. The party had materialized.

Then someone asked if I had any songs of my own that I could sing. I have hundreds of songs, but I did not feel that I was supposed to "preach" to these people with any of them. Desperately searching my mental jukebox of Bob Kilpatrick songs, I realized I had written a song for my kids that was heartwarming but not explicitly spiritual. So I introduced the song "Happy Family" and sang:

> *Green fields, trees against the sky,*
> *Children running by me,*
> *It's my four boys, laughing as they play,*
> *Making my heart so very glad.*
> *Then I hear their mama call, "Supper's on the table,*
> *Come wash your hands and settle down to eat."*
> *There's a tear in my eye, I'm happy to be*
> *The daddy of this happy family.*
> *Ooh, it's so good to have a happy family.*
> *You can have a happy family too.*
> *I may never be rich enough*
> *To give my family all that they desire.*
> *But I know we'll have plenty of*
> *The things that make a home full of love.*

Just as I finished the song, a little chime went off and the seat-belt light indicated we were in our final approach to our destination. As we exited the plane, I was surrounded by people thanking me for the wonderful experience on the flight. Even the drunk guy had been touched. The man picking me up at the airport was stunned by all the people shaking my hand and talking about the onboard concert. There had been no altar call or moment of decision. But God had displayed me to those people in a way that suited his purposes in their lives.

A COMMUNITY OF WITNESSES

The Christian community, by definition, is a collection of artworks in progress. We are a community that is— or should be—rooted in the love that God uses to draw people to himself. It is the most irresistible kind of community on the planet. Love, by its nature, is evangelistic. It welcomes and even compels people to belong.

I know this firsthand because it was a loving community that caused me to become a committed follower of Jesus. I was seventeen, living in Los Angeles, and auditioning for the musical *Hair.* I had moved there to make a career as an actor after traveling the country for five months in a repertory theater group that was "Christian" but whose members were—I am not kidding—a Buddhist convert, two members of the Weather Underground Organization terrorist group, a guy who was increasingly interested in becoming a warlock, and a girl who slept with a different guy at every place we stopped. Clearly, this was not the kind of Christian community I was looking for.

I had left the group to bunk down at a friend's apartment in LA. I owned next to nothing. The cupboard was bare except for a box of Shredded Wheat and a bottle of yellow mustard, both three months old. But things were going to change because I had received my big break: I had been granted an audition for the Los Angeles premier of *Hair*—which meant that I was guaranteed a part in the production. It was just a matter of which part they would give me.

But the day I was scheduled to try out for a major role, I received a letter from my dad that stated, in essence, "Son, come home." I think he knew what kind of lifestyle I was living, what kind of people I was hanging around, and how poor I was, not just financially but spiritually. I was sitting in a parked car outside the theater with a friend, waiting for my call time. I reread the letter and decided on the spot to skip the audition and go home. My dad bought me an airplane ticket, and I left LA to head home.

A major surprise awaited me.

My family had dramatically changed—in fact, it was in the midst of genuine revival, the kind familiar to anyone who went through the Jesus movement or a charismatic renewal. They were having church services in our living room where people danced and sang, "The Holy Ghost will set your feet a dancin'. The Holy Ghost will fill you through and through." Returning home, I saw a community more vibrant than I had ever seen. I felt their love and joy. It was overwhelming and real, and I wanted it. I had to belong. I made the decision right then to abandon all other pursuits in life and follow Jesus. I did not do this because of a tract or an argument. My dad didn't sit me down and say, "Now, Bobby, it's time to get your priorities in order." I did it because my heart longed to join the authentic community of believers and to have the kind of joyful relationship with Jesus that I saw in them.

One of the deepest cries of the human heart is to belong to a supportive, challenging community in which our "art"—ourselves—is developed. In God's community, we're transformed by the Master Artist into lasting masterpieces.

This is how evangelism works: loving relationships are magnetic. God loves us. We love him and each other— and that is the most powerful force on earth.

Witness isn't a verb; it's who you are. Start *being*. Be together. Love. Remember, God has already got you on display.

6

ART AND
OUR PERSONAL
LIMITATIONS

So free we seem, so fettered fast we are!

Robert Browning, poet

Art is limitation. The essence of every picture is
the frame.

G. K. Chesterton

Never judge a work of art by its defects.

Washington Allston, nineteenth-century

American Romantic painter

C indy and I made our way through the labyrinthine corridors in the massive Louvre Museum in Paris. Anyone who has been there knows how breathtakingly large this complex of buildings is. With its countless exhibits, it would take weeks to give everything the attention it deserves. Like most visitors, however, we had only a day to spend, and our particular goal—like every other tourist in Paris that day—was to see da Vinci's *Mona Lisa*, arguably the most famous painting in the world.

Just getting to the *Mona Lisa* is like taking a day hike through the history of art. We passed through sculpture rooms; we saw native artifacts in glass cases, Renaissance art with great gilded frames, and much more. At last we made it to the end of an especially long, sunlit hallway adorned with priceless oil paintings. There to the right, in its own grand alcove, was the *Mona Lisa*—and I almost laughed out loud at the mismatch between reality and my expectations. The painting is a mere thirty inches by twenty inches, and it looked positively diminutive, even after we pushed our way through crowds and stood as close as we could.

Similarly, van Gogh's famous *Starry Night* (on display at the Museum of Modern Art in New York) is three feet by two and a half feet—probably smaller than your bathroom mirror. Some of our greatest works of art are no bigger than placemats. The works of the masters hang so large in our collective imagination that to see them in person can be underwhelming at first. Yet on these small stretches of canvas and wood, great stories were told and history was made. The size of each painting did not matter as much as the painting itself.

All art—especially the best art—is necessarily defined by its limitations. Every canvas has a border, and every song has a beginning and an end. In fact, the edge of the canvas or the end of a song or play is of primary importance and must be considered from the very start for the artist to do his best work. We, too, as God's works of art, are created to be great in spite of, and even because of, our limitations. God has expressed himself uniquely in each of us, and he uses our limitations to bring himself glory.

Every life—indeed, every created thing—has boundaries. Our bodies take up only so much space and can be just one place at a time. We have limited intelligence and strength. Our days have a beginning and an end. We all have a certain height and weight, health issues, eyesight, and so on. Just as we would never accept that all paintings must conform to some arbitrary canvas size regulation, so we must recognize that God has the freedom to express himself uniquely in each of us. He wants to tell a certain part of his great story in our lives—and limitations are a necessary and natural part of that story.

As we stood in the Louvre contemplating the *Mona Lisa*, it was easy to see what was there. It was painted on a panel of poplar, with a muted palette of greens and browns. A road wound through the background behind the subject's famously enigmatic smile. But what struck me was what was missing from it. It was simply a portrait of a woman. There was no starry sky or van Gogh's bold brushes of color. There were none of Monet's startling chromatic city scenes or haystacks. There was no evidence of Rembrandt's way with light and shadow.

But does the *Mona Lisa* suffer from what it is missing? Do we enjoy it any less because there are no haystacks or stars? No, because each person, and each painting, is a window into the imagination of the artist. We see through his eyes the part of his world that he wishes to show us. What the artist includes and excludes, and how he frames it, helps him tell a certain story. In the same way, God is telling a story through you.

ACCEPTING OUR OWN LIMITATIONS

I don't like borders. Like most people, I don't want to be pigeonholed. When someone refers to me as a musician I want to remind them that I'm also a speaker. When they refer to me as a radio personality, I want to say that I'm a record producer too — and I write books!

A few years ago, it occurred to me that I was trying to live as though my canvas had no border. I was trying to be Bob the Renaissance man, but I felt more like a mediocre piece of art. Art that tries to be limitless ends up being useless. That's why God doesn't mind our limitations. In fact, he created us with limitations that serve as the boundaries of his great art. Our limitations are the frame for God's amazing creativity.

When I first started experimenting with recording, all I had was a four-track cassette recorder and a drum sequencer. I was influenced in my early approach by Bruce Springsteen's *Dakota* album, which was also recorded on a four-track cassette machine. What struck me most was that Springsteen had played to the limitations of his recording medium and made a powerful album that didn't pretend to be anything but what it was. The lesson to me was simple: use your limitations to tell your story. If you deny your limitations and try to make your four-track song sound as though it was recorded on forty-eight tracks at Abbey Road Studios in London, you're working against the power of your art and you'll likely embarrass yourself. Embracing your limitations is the only way to make an honest and true piece of art.

As I was growing up, certain people repeatedly told me, "You can do anything you want." Only much later, and after many disappointments, did I realize this was a terrible, if well-intentioned, lie. I can't do anything I want, no matter how hard I try. And neither can you. Rather, God has outfitted each of us with a few certain things we can do well. He has put boundaries on us.

It is no surprise, then, that some of the worst times in our lives come when we try to work outside our border and pursue a dream that doesn't match the Artist's vision. It complicates things when our dream is similar to our natural talents. When I first started in music, I wanted to be one of the guys my age I saw on Christian album covers. They had bands; I wanted a band! They rocked; I wanted to rock! They had agents and managers and labels and hairstylists. I had my kitchen table and a telephone, and I kicked against the constraints of my life. I wanted to conform myself to the image of these stars, but God had something else in mind—something better for me. I am sorry to say that it took me years to make peace with my place in the ministry.

The Bible says we are foolish to compare ourselves to each other. The apostle Paul used the picture of the body to teach the Corinthians that diversity in gifts was something to delight in. "If the whole body were an eye," he says, "where would be the hearing?" (1 Corinthians 12:17). So it may surprise you, as it did me, that God is not waiting for us to overcome our limitations. In fact, God does his best work within what seem to be our most debilitating limitations. Think of the cross. Think of what Jesus told Paul: "My grace is sufficient for you, for My strength is made perfect in weakness" (2 Corinthians 12:9).

Notice that Jesus did not say, "My strength is made perfect when you have enough faith to conquer your weaknesses." Or, "My strength will be made perfect once I have worked these mistakes out of your life."

What Jesus said was, "My strength is made perfect in weakness."

You can't get more anti-math than that.

As a music producer, I have learned that there are limits to the kinds of music I can produce. These limitations make me a great fit for some musicians and a wrong choice for others. I tend to gravitate toward simple, guitar-based music. I don't do many expansive orchestrations, "diva pop," or electronic sequencing (except when it's appropriate for the song). I've had wonderful experiences with a number of artists, but also my share of mismatches in the recording process. It is excruciating to see a project all the way through to the end when I and the artist both know that his or her artistic vision is outside my limitations. That's why I began having extensive conversations with potential artists, not so much to discover how I would work with them, but whether I should work with them at all. Knowing my limitations and the shape of my canvas, and knowing when to say no, made my life much better and allowed me to work with those I could really help.

We are at our best when we work within our frame, and sometimes it takes someone else to tell us this. These rebukes are seldom welcome, but they can be life chang-

ing and good. I was a music pastor for a couple of years—
a *bad* music pastor. I loved the people, but I had no heart
for the kind of responsibilities the church leaders wanted
me to undertake. One day, Rev. Earl Johnson at Bethel
Church in Redding, California, called me into his office.
I felt like I was coming to the throne of judgment. He told
me what I was good at and what I was not good at. He
wasn't being mean—he simply loved me. He had taken
my measure and knew better than I did which ministry
would suit me best. He offered the full support of the
church while I launched into itinerant music ministry.
And he continued to be a great supporter of my ministry,
sometimes praising and other times correcting me. He
helped me to live artfully within my limitations, to see
the frame and boundaries of my life.

J. B. Phillips translates Paul in Romans 12:3 as stating
that we should have "a sane estimate" of our capabilities.
In other words, God calls us to understand our limits,
live within them, and rejoice in what he will do in us and
through us.

LIMITATIONS
CREATE BEAUTY

Limitations are a necessary and unavoidable part of the
beauty God is creating in us. I quoted G. K. Chesterton at the beginning of this chapter: "Art is limitation.

The essence of every picture is the frame." Robert Frost famously said that writing poetry without rhyme and meter is like playing tennis without a net.

As a composer, I often set strict limitations for myself before I begin writing a song just to see if I can make something beautiful of it. I limit the number of chords I use, or closely mimic the style of another composer, or specify what instruments the song will use or how "wordy" it will be. I have found that the most memorable songs I have written are the ones on which I placed strong borders. For example, my best-known song, "Lord, Be Glorified," uses only five notes in the chorus. It is almost embarrassingly simple—and yet lovely. Another popular song I wrote, "I Will Not Be Ashamed," has only two chords in the whole song. That's right—two chords—and the song can go on for a half hour and still feel fresh. In both songs the frame enhances their art and makes them what they are.

So it is easy for me to picture God setting limitations on each of us when he conceived us before the world began. Our so-called "weaknesses" are built in. They were God's idea.

But we need to make one thing clear: when I talk about limitations and weaknesses, I am not talking about sinful habits or life-controlling problems. God will probably not work through your drinking problem or your adultery (except in a redemptive way, which is a different thing).

I am talking about those areas where we feel we don't measure up, where we don't have the "talent" that others have—and even those areas where we feel bedeviled or tormented by some besetting problem or tendency. This type of thorn in the flesh was what Paul was struggling with when the Lord stated that his power is made perfect in weakness. And it seems to be what prompted Paul to embrace his own limitations, so he could say:

"If I must boast, I will boast of the things that show my weakness" (2 Corinthians 11:30 NIV).

"I will not boast about myself, except about my weaknesses" (2 Corinthians 12:5 NIV).

"Therefore I will boast all the more gladly about my weaknesses, so that Christ's power may rest on me" (2 Corinthians 12:9 NIV).

Paul understood that in the kingdom, strength can be weakness, and weakness strength. So he was not ashamed to speak freely of his own limitations. He wrote, "We, however, will not boast beyond proper limits, but will confine our boasting to the field God has assigned to us, a field that reaches even to you.... Neither do we go beyond our limits by boasting of work done by others" (2 Corinthians 10:13, 15 NIV).

This is the apostle's graceful and wise way of acknowledging the truth: that God has given us healthy parameters in our lives, and we are happiest when we allow him to create our art within them.

ACCEPTING LIMITATIONS
GIVES US PEACE

Only when we accept who we are, flaws and all, will we have peace. Every now and then, I hear a new version of the same old "prosperity" message: God has not intended us to have any boundaries in our lives at all, so if we'll just rebuke the devil and trust God, we will be given riches, power, favor, health, and anything else we want. The reason goes that if we have an illness or disease and we aren't healed, there must be something wrong in our lives.

This is plainly math—and plainly unbiblical. It's a desperate search for the debit in the sin column that will account for the defect and make sense to us. It's an attempt to reject all discomfort, displeasure, and suffering; to push away the hands of God from the clay of our lives; to limit the ways in which he can form us into the image of Jesus. Many of these "overcomers" are fond of quoting Philippians 4:13, "I can do all things through Christ who strengthens me." But they get the meaning of the passage precisely wrong. Paul was not speaking of being delivered *from* all constraints and limitations, but of being content *in the midst of* all constraints and limitations. Whether he was comfortable or not, Paul was confident that Jesus would strengthen him *within* the limitations God places on him. That is the message of art.

Every few years I hear a new story of someone with a significant disability who overcomes it to live a full life. There was Helen Keller, who became blind and deaf at nineteen months. There are people missing arms or legs, or even all their limbs, who learn to do things we would consider impossible, like play instruments and drive cars. We are moved when we see what these people can do and especially that they are joyful and fulfilled. What moves us except the realization that God has made great art within a very limited frame? Their overcoming is not of the miraculous variety—growing their limbs again or receiving their sight or hearing—but of the kind that works wonderfully and creatively within the sometimes unbelievably restrictive boundaries placed on them.

How many things are you praying for right now that are beyond your border? How many frustrations are you feeling because you are concerned about something outside the frame of your canvas? How many times have you tried to be limitless or wished that your limitations matched those of someone else?

The way of art takes delight in the way God has made us, knowing that he is working within the limits of our lives to make something beautiful of us. Paul could glory in his weakness rather than just accept it begrudgingly. Only an artistic understanding of life could allow him to say this. Accepting that we have weaknesses and limitations gives us the opportunity to open the door and invite

God into them. We allow him to remove, or change, or, surprisingly, even use them.

Think back to the last time you lost yourself in a painting, song, or play. Within each work of art is what appears to be a limitless expanse. We feel that, in the painting, there is a world just over the horizon that we could journey to if we could only enter into the canvas. Novels present whole universes of people and places that engage our minds as if they were real. And music—the best music—takes us to a place that is timeless. Accepting that the canvas of our lives has an edge does not mean that we are "settling for less"; it means we are settling *in* to our God-designed borders, ready to watch the Master Artist paint his boundless story on our lives.

ACCEPTING THE
LIMITATIONS OF OTHERS

Most of the famous paintings Cindy and I saw in Paris were irregular in their dimensions. There was no mass production back then. Each frame was likely handmade by the artist, so each was unique in size and construction. The materials they used varied widely as well. There are paintings on many kinds of canvas, wood, and even stone. Many artists mixed their own paints with natural pigments they found in plants and animals, so there are as many reds, blues, yellows, and greens as there are paintings. Some canvases are so thick with paint as to be nearly three-dimensional, while others are done in thin washes of color. Some artists painted over previous efforts—marvelously revealed in recent years through the use of infrared reflectography (which is a wonderful sermon on redemption that I'll let you preach to yourself).

In the same way, each of us is handmade by God, and knowing this helps us appreciate the people around us in a new way. Accepting that each of us is limited by design gives us the freedom to enjoy who people *are* rather than wish they were different. Our callings, abilities, proclivities, and placements differ, but there is an artistic vision for each of us. We need each other exactly as God made us to be. To demand that people be something other than themselves is as futile as putting on a country album and expecting to hear a Mozart piano concerto.

Fighting against the limitations of others is a bad business. It causes all sorts of strife as they fail to meet our improper expectations. But once we accept another person's boundaries, we can enjoy what is within them and discover there a world somehow more vast than the space allowed by the frame. Concentrating on the edges of the frame and being disappointed by its size or shape always lead to disappointment. But when you focus on the artwork *within the frame*, you become lost in that world. Isn't this why we go to museums anyway? To peer through the windows of time into one world after another? Isn't this why we people-watch—to glimpse the greatness of the Artist in the glorious variety of his artwork?

Jesus affirmed people's unique place and calling wherever he went. He commended the Roman centurion's great faith, spoke kindly to the Pharisee Nicodemus, and sent the delivered demoniac back to his village rather than allowing him to join the rank of his disciples. The wonderful subtext of all this is that he created us for unity, not uniformity!

Most fans of the Beatles were taken aback by the mediocrity of Paul's early solo recordings on which he played every instrument and sang every part. The drumming was lackluster, the guitar work perfunctory, and the harmonies stiff. I wondered if he really didn't hear how thin it was. I dreamed about what the songs might have sounded like if John, George, and Ringo had played on them—how the push and pull between the Lads would have enriched the songs. The songwriting partnership of John Lennon and Paul McCartney worked only as long as they valued the strengths *and weaknesses* of the other. After the Beatles broke up, John famously belittled Paul for filling the world with silly love songs. Paul took the line and made a hit song out of it, asking, "But what's wrong with that?" Both of them were describing the edges of Paul's artwork. Silly love songs are where Paul shone. The Beatles' two most popular songs of all time are "Yesterday" and "Michelle," both written by

Paul and both ballads. If John (and Paul) had continued to accept and take delight in that "limitation," it might have made their friendship a bit less rocky, and the world would have had even more love songs (and what's wrong with that?). Every Beatle fan knows that Paul alone could become treacly and John alone could become caustic. But together, their limitations balanced the limitations of the other, and their songs were rich and full.

Paradoxically, the purpose of our limitations is glory. The Bible tells us that God wants the whole earth to be filled with his glory. "But truly, as I live, all the earth shall be filled with the glory of the LORD" (Numbers 14:21). "And let the whole earth be filled with His glory" (Psalm 72:19).

Some Christians see glory as a mystical nexus between earth and heaven — an overwhelming sense of God's power or a kind of swirling, dizzying cloud of his presence. Others believe that nature is God's ultimate expression of his glory. But I have come to believe that God's greatest glory is in people — flawed, human, limited people. As the Bible tells us, mankind is the crowning achievement of God's creation (Psalm 8:4–8; Hebrews 2:5–8). God told the first humans to be fruitful and multiply — to fill the world with humans, which sounds a lot like "let the whole earth be filled with His glory." If mankind is truly the glory of the Lord, we ought to look for his glory in each other. This should change our perspective considerably. We should take great delight in each others' eccentricities and limitations because we are looking for a certain reflection of Jesus in every face— the glory of the Lord. And as Paul said, his glory can be most evident in our weaknesses.

This means that the next time you notice something about a friend or family member that rankles you, remember that God's strength can be made perfect in that weakness. You may be glimpsing God's glory in that person's limitation. When you see someone who has a temper, consider that God may desire to use that trait to help the poor or call people away from sin. If a friend of yours seems like a pushover, perhaps God wants, through him, to give comfort and compassion to people who've hit rock bottom.

God will use each of us, in all our weaknesses and limitations, when we surrender to him. The way of art is to say, "I will therefore glory in my weakness, for in my weakness, God is strong."

A STRANGE DAY
AT CHURCH

My friend Brent Jameson was the worship pastor at a church southeast of Portland, Oregon, that met in a historic sanctuary among the trees on the foothills of Mount Hood. It was a beautifully handcrafted building with room for just seventy-five people.

On Wednesdays, Brent would ask the Father what he wanted to hear from his children the following Sunday, planning the song service with a listening ear to his voice. One Wednesday, Brent felt that God asked him to lead the old hymn "In the Garden." But Brent had never liked that song. He thought it sounded whiny and sentimental —and besides, only old people sang it. So he decided to skip it.

The next Wednesday, Brent felt the same tender urging toward the song again. In fact, all week there were subtle echoes of this suggestion. It seemed people were humming it or talking about it everywhere he went. Still, he would not lead it.

The third Wednesday, he felt the same urging. Not only that, but his mother mentioned that she wanted "In the Garden" sung at her funeral. Then a flower arrangement arrived with a little ceramic hymnbook opened permanently to that same song. Finally—and with a bit of grumbling—Brent gave in.

Sunday morning came, and the sanctuary was nearly filled to its seventy-five-person capacity. When he invited the congregation to open their tattered old hymnbooks to "In the Garden," a man in the fourth row let out a whoop of joy that startled them all.

When they started to sing, this fellow, who appeared to be drunk, stood up and sang loudly from memory in a voice that sounded like Nutty Professor-era Jerry Lewis.

The fellow sang every word of every verse and between the lyrics would whoop and hoot excitedly. When the song ended, he yelled, "You guys are great! I love you so much!" and sat down.

Brent, with his eyes on the visitor, said, "We're going to sing just one more song this morning, one you may remember from Sunday school. Let's sing 'Jesus Loves Me.'"

The drunk visitor let out another holler and shouted, "This is for *me*!" As the congregation began to sing, the visitor jumped up on the pew and began to dance as he sang, all the while whooping between the words. At the close of the song, the man shouted, "You guys are great! I love you so much! Thank you! Thank you so much!" and sat down. Brent closed in prayer and left the stage perplexed as the visitor clapped and shouted for more.

As Brent came down the stairs, his friend Judy met him and said, "I feel I should explain to you what just happened." They went into a back room and got a cup of coffee, and she told Brent the backstory.

The "drunk" man's name was Randall. As a teenager, he had stopped leaving his home because of debilitating agoraphobia (the fear of public places). He hardly even came out of his room for meals. He lived like that for twenty years. Over time, his family situation changed enough that he could no longer stay at home. He was taken to a care facility where he lived for fourteen more years. Judy's son, Frank, was assigned to be Randall's therapist.

When they first met, Randall hardly acknowledged Frank. He wouldn't speak or look at him. Frank stuck with him, though, and kept seeing him week after week, talking and attempting to engage him and draw him out.

It began to have an effect. Randall gave him a slight wave of greeting one week. Another week he said hello. A few weeks later, Randall introduced himself. Soon they were talking like friends.

One week, Frank walked in and Randall told him, "I want to go out." This was real progress. Frank said, "That's great, Randall! I'll help you. I'll go with you. In fact, why don't you go with me to church?"

This suggestion agitated Randall. "I've never been to church! I don't know what they do there." Frank tried to reassure him. "Oh, it's very simple. We sing some songs together, the pastor speaks to us, and we go home."

"I don't know any church songs!" said Randall.

"I'll teach you a couple," said Frank.

"Today," Judy told Brent, "is the day. This is Randall's first time out in public in thirty-four years. For *two years* Frank and Randall have been preparing for this day. And for two years Frank has been teaching Randall two songs: 'In the Garden' and 'Jesus Loves Me.'"

If you think this is just a crazy coincidence, like seeing your junior high math teacher at Disney World, then you should take this book right back to the store and get a refund. This book is not for you.

Rather, I hope you see how the God of love was at work in Randall's life and in Randall's limitations. God's art is so important to him that he precisely orchestrated this special day just for Randall. He did not size up Randall's limitations, examine his canvas, and dismiss him because there wasn't enough room to work. He doesn't treat anyone like that.

God used Brent's limitations too—his reluctance to yield and include the song for several weeks. He knew just how to press on his heart to make sure he sang those two songs on that very Sunday—and not one week sooner or later. He used Brent's weakness to make great art for Randall.

God will work wonders within your frame too. He loves you as much as he loves Randall. What God did for him, he will do for you. When you yield to him in humble recognition of your weakness and limitations, he will show off his dazzling ideas on the canvas of your life.

THE ART
OF SACRIFICE

He who would accomplish little
must sacrifice little; he who would achieve
much must sacrifice much; he who would
attain highly must sacrifice greatly.
James Allen, author and poet

A life of sacrifice is the pinnacle of art,
and is full of true joy.
Gandhi

Artists must be sacrificed to their art.
Ralph Waldo Emerson

Art requires sacrifice—but not the kind we might assume. It has nothing to do with money. It is not a sacrifice of time, energy, emotional investment, or knowledge. It is something different and something more.

I have twice visited the temple of Kali, the goddess of death, near the Ganges River in Calcutta, India. The air there is heavy with exhaust fumes, industrial smog, and the mingling odors you would expect of a city of thirteen million people and at least that many cows and goats.

On my first visit, I stepped into the courtyard of the temple and saw a newly sacrificed goat laying to the side while a young man stood in its spilled blood, holding the blood-covered horns of the altar and putting his head between them, where, only moments before, the goat's throat had been slit open and drained. An old priest chanted a purification incantation over him before demanding an offering.

Fifty feet down the dirty street stands a plain two-story building where for sixty years Mother Teresa lived and worked at the Home for the Destitute and Dying. Inside, the Sisters of Mercy take away the rags of the beggars and dress them in clean clothes. They cleanse their open sores, place them on comfortable beds, feed them, and care for them until they die. When the beggars need a doctor, they are taken to the Mission of Mercy hospital, started by my friend, the late Mark Buntain. He and his wife, Huldah, gave themselves, as Mother Teresa did, to the City of Kali, knowing that the people to whom they minister would never be able to repay them.

In both Kali's temple and Mother Teresa's home, a sacrifice is being offered up. One is an exchange, the other a gift. One is made to appease the goddess of death and is dead itself, while the other is a living sacrifice in the name of the Living God who delights in the sacrificial acts of devotion done for "the least of these" in the name of Jesus.

Sacrifice makes no sense. It is as non-math as you can get. But art involves sacrifice in important ways that illuminate our relationship with God. The way we perceive sacrifice, and how we respond to it, makes all the difference in what we end up being.

I have given plenty of sacrifices in my life. No, I didn't bring a goat to be slaughtered at the temple. But as I mentioned earlier, I did spend many hours at the altar praying and confessing my sins to God, hoping he would forgive me again. Is this much different from the man in the temple of Kali? It seems to me that I was wanting a new sacrifice every time I needed mercy. This is plainly math. I compared the credit and debit columns of my life and tried to zero them out as much as possible each day. I was like a grocery store employee counting up the register before going home. O, foolish Galatian! Who has bewitched you? Having begun with art, will you now finish with math?

God has not called us to *give* a sacrifice, but to *be* a sacrifice. The book of Hebrews, a virtual treatise on the art of sacrifice, tells us in chapter 9 that offering an animal in sacrifice is an earthly picture of a heavenly reality, an enactment of a sacrifice that happened there once for all. Hebrews says about it that if we constantly needed a new sacrifice "[Jesus] then would have had to suffer often since the foundation of the world" (9:26).

But Hebrews goes on to make it clear that Jesus suffered *once* for all and there is no need for him "to suffer often." And just as Jesus has offered himself, he calls us to offer ourselves—not to *make* a sacrifice, which we would need to do repeatedly, but to *become* one.

A PROCESS OF SACRIFICE

Any artist can testify that art involves sacrifice. Making art is not always a happy process. It can be hard and unpleasant. The artist pours everything—and more—into the work. I often joke during a concert that I "play" for a living. Nobody ever says to me, "Bob, work me a song." They say, "Bob, play me a song." Naturally, I don't mention the hundreds of hours spent in the studio at my home writing, recording, wrestling with a melody or a lyric, and practicing. This is the hard work that lets me "play," and that makes what I do into art.

What makes you and me great as God's works of art is not just what he has put into us but what he doesn't allow to remain. He is editing us down. The Bible calls it pruning. To put it in terms of filmmaking, some of our ambitions, habits, and opinions are going to end up on the cutting-room floor. God is, as they used to say in Hollywood, cutting to the chase. He is bringing out the parts in us that are special and unique.

My *Time Out with Bob Kilpatrick* radio devotional is one minute long. I have sixty seconds in which to communicate and inspire. If I said everything about a subject that I had in my mind, the program would be two or three hours long each day!

Some of my most well-known songs have undergone significant changes before reaching their final form. I wrote a song called "Here Am I (Send Me to the Nations)." It came to me as I was stepping out onto the stage at a youth conference in Canada in the mid-eighties. It was an appropriate message for the people there that night, so I sang it, and over the years it became a favorite call to missions worldwide. Years later, the fellow who did sound at the conference sent me a Christmas gift—the original cassette recording of that song from the night of its birth. I listened to it and was struck by how much the song had changed from that first rendition to the finished version. I don't even remember changing it, but I had tweaked the phrasing, timing, and melody. It's a better song for it. Had I left it as it was, perhaps the song would have served a purpose that night but not beyond that. As it is, the song became a useful tool in God's hands and has been one of the most popular songs I've ever written.

I'm reminded of what da Vinci said: "Thou, O God, dost sell us all good things at the price of labor."[1]

I have another song called "Nails in the Hands of a Carpenter," which I have written three times. That is, I have three completely different versions of the same song. The first two are OK, but they lacked wit and did not communicate what I was trying to say. Six years after conceiving of the idea, I finally had an idea for the lyrics of version number three:

> *It wasn't a pen in the hands of a poet that caused my*
> *heart to sing*
> *It wasn't a brush in the hands of a painter that drew me*
> *to the King*
> *And it wasn't a sword in the hands of a soldier that set*
> *my spirit free*
> *It was greater than these, it was nails in the hands of*
> *a carpenter*

It wasn't a coin in the hands of a merchant that
  purchased me with gold
It wasn't a scepter in the courts of a king that bid me
  come so bold
It wasn't a net in the hands of a fisher that caught my
  floundering soul
It was greater than these, it was nails in the hands of
  a carpenter

(bridge) Oh the wood of the cross and the hammer
  they used
Were tools of the carpenter's trade
And when they put the nails in His hands that day
It meant my debt was paid

It wasn't the words of a thundering prophet that washed
  me like the rain
It wasn't the gifts of three wandering wise men that
  turned my loss to gain
It wasn't the touch of the hands of a surgeon that eased
  my spirit's pain
It was greater than these, it was nails in the hands of
  a carpenter
And if you believe, you're so thankful for nails in
  the hands
Nails in the hands of a carpenter

These wordplays pleased me: "brush ... painter ...
drew," "net ... fisher ... floundering soul," "thundering

prophet ... washed ... rain." I had many other ideas that never made it to the song, but I sacrificed them for the overall benefit of the song.

I tell songwriters that I want to hear the sweat in their songs. If they don't work it over and over again until every word and note is right, they're not making the sacrifice necessary for great art.

When producing a recording, I typically throw many more instruments and vocals on the tracks than I eventually use. I often record three or four takes of the lead vocal. I then make a composite track from the various takes to make one "super vocal." I'll listen to the song and try to find which instruments are sitting well in the song. Sometimes I'll even rerecord a part months after having laid down the original. I suppose you could say I use a reductive approach to producing. Even in writing this book I see that it is the editing, the paring of whole sections, that has focused and sharpened the message. If we had kept everything I wrote, the book would be twice as long—and you would most likely be terribly bored with it! I have found in this a corollary to my own life. My life will seem to be full of opportunities, interests, and personal abilities. I find sometimes that I have walked through every door that has opened to me. And then God begins to close them. One by one he pulls things from the musical track of my life that aren't sitting well. He cuts whole sections out. They may be good, but they don't enhance the art in the way he wants.

Artists must be ruthless with their art. In a divinely inspired moment, Michelangelo said of his sculpting, "I saw the angel in the marble and carved until I set him free." So God sees the saint in you and will not stop until it is fully freed from all that obscures it.

DIRECTOR'S CUT

The struggle comes when we disagree with God over what should be cut out. We develop an affection for something that he knows will compromise the beauty of who we are. We lean on our own understanding, believing our perspective to be the best and our information the most reliable. Like Jacob, we wrestle with the angel instead of trusting him.

Have you ever seen a movie that just felt too long? It was a good story, but the filmmakers tried to put too much in there, and in the end it just dragged? They tried to create an epic when a simple romance would have sufficed? Some people live like this. They are unwilling to let God edit them. I sometimes watch the director's cut of a film when I rent the DVD. Rare is the time when I think the film is better for being longer. Seeing the director's version makes me grateful for the studio boss who made them cut it down for theatrical release.

Of course, the director sees things differently. He feels the edits violate the basic integrity of his idea. You probably feel the same way at times about the edits in your life. Who hasn't come to a place where they were asked to give up something they always took for granted that they would have? Sometimes the cut goes too deep and is too central to who we believe we are. We can't imagine that God would take this or that away, so we resist, sometimes blindly.

Recently I decided that the time had come for me to stop producing recording projects other than my own. I had wanted to be a producer for so long and had put together a very nice studio full of equipment and instruments. I had worked with some of the top Christian musicians. But I found that I was enjoying it less and less. When I made the decision to stop, however, I was amazed at how difficult it was. It had come very near the core of my self-image, and to give it up was to remove what seemed like a foundation stone in my life.

We have an example in sacrifice. Jesus gave the greatest sacrifice any human will ever give. He didn't want to. He told the Father so, but then he allowed the Father to edit away his desires and to make the kind of artwork he wanted. The crucifixion was the highest art—the promise of redemption and remaking of creation, the Artist becoming one with his art, redeeming it from within and sacrificing so it could be fully realized.

What seems like a sacrifice will, paradoxically, always add more than it takes away. The Impressionist painter Georges Seurat "sacrificed" his time in long hours watching the sea on sentry duty in what must have felt like wasted time; but this became invaluable when he later painted the sea better than almost anyone. Monet's budding artistic career was interrupted by his conscription into the army to serve in Algeria. What looked like an awful disruption turned into the very experience that made him a revolutionary painter, for in Algeria he began to see light differently. "You cannot imagine to what an extent I increased my knowledge and how much my vision gained thereby," he said later. "I did not quite realize it at first. The impressions of light and color that I received there were not to classify themselves until later; but they contained the germ of my future researches."[2]

He was forced onto the road of sacrifice—and there he gained his greatest insight.

You cannot be God's art if you will not sacrifice. There is no director's cut in heaven. In a mysterious way, we are like the burning bush Moses encountered in Exodus 3. We burn but are not consumed. We die and yet we live. We lose our lives only to find them again. We give ourselves away and discover that God has given us back our true selves, purified.

On the road of sacrifice it will sometimes seem to you as though God hates you and is punishing you. You may even get the impression that he is trying to destroy you; but this is a lie. He wants you to live! The Artist is simply taking away everything that doesn't belong in his masterpiece.

Once again we find ourselves speaking of mysteries with this paradoxical idea of a "living sacrifice." J. B. Phillips paraphrases so wonderfully what Paul states in Romans 12:1–2 that it bears quoting in its full context:

> With eyes wide open to the mercies of God, I beg you, my brothers, as an act of intelligent worship, to give him your bodies, as a living sacrifice, consecrated to him and acceptable by him. Don't let the world around you squeeze you into its own mould, but let God re-mould your minds from within, so that you may prove in practice that the plan of God for you is good, meets all his demands and moves towards the goal of true maturity.

REAL SACRIFICE

Let me be clear about what sacrifice is not.

Sacrifice Is Not Destruction

I was sitting in front of the fireplace with my guitar on my lap one evening when I was a young man. I had begun to minister in music and had committed my life to

Jesus. However, music had become more than a means for sharing the gospel for me; it had become a point of pride and ambition. As I looked into the fire, I struggled with the question of which would have the upper hand in my life, God or music. After more than an hour of considering the matter deeply on that couch, I took my guitar, smashed it in half over my knee, and threw it into the fire. Music would not rule my life—God would. I watched the guitar burn to ash.

That was a sacrifice I needed to make at that moment. It was an expression of devotion to Christ. I was also a young man, and young men—especially spiritual young men—are given to dramatic acts. But this is not what I mean when talking about sacrifice. The fact is, I soon acquired a new guitar and continued ministering in song. God would not let something be destroyed that was part of his artistic vision for me.

Sacrifice is not destruction. I have heard preachers misuse John the Baptist's words, "He must increase, but I must decrease" (John 3:30), as a proof text for what sounded to me like God's desire to annihilate the uniqueness of who I am. In many sermons and testimonies over the years, they seemed to be saying that God wants to destroy us and make us nothing. What kind of art would that be?

As I write this, I am sitting by the fireplace in my office

and occasionally adding logs to the fire, then brushing off my hands before I type. I am a little older and (I hope) less dramatic, but I would gladly break any of my guitars over my knee and burn them if I felt the Lord wanted that. It would give me great joy to do so, if it gave him great joy. But that is not what artistic sacrifice is. As I listen to the comforting sound of crackling wood as it is consumed by the flame, I think of the many times we believers fear that God's fire will consume us too. We think that if we surrender ourselves to him, we will end up a pile of ash.

Of course, this isn't true. Art's ultimate purpose is to create, not destroy. God's fire refines us and makes us stronger. Cindy and I have a friend we've known for many years, and for a long time she was a potter. She made household items like mugs and lamps out of clay. The pieces were beautiful—true works of art. She had a workplace in her basement with a throwing wheel and a kiln. Over the years, I have sipped hundreds of gallons of coffee from the mugs she made, and they remain among the most lovely and useful in my embarrassingly large collection of coffee mugs. The lamps she made still light various rooms in our house.

But if she had ever decided not to fire her creations in the kiln—letting them dry out on a shelf instead—they wouldn't have lasted a week. The brittle clay would have cracked at the slightest bump. Our friend fired her pieces in the kiln because she wanted them to be beautiful and strong.

In short, she fired her creations in order to save them.

Sacrifice Is Not Guilt

One of my pet peeves is songs or sermons that motivate with guilt. I produced an album one time for a fellow who had a song about the wonderful sacrifice Jesus made for us on the cross. In the bridge he wanted to introduce another theme, which was, "If God did this for you, why won't you do more for him?" It introduced the motivation of guilt. I tried to skirt the issue or subtly suggest that he could write a better lyric, but he kept coming back with the same message in a new form. I finally told him that I couldn't agree with the point of the lyric. If Jesus, "who for the joy that was set before Him endured the cross, despising the shame" (Hebrews 12:2), then how could I feel any differently about it than Jesus did? If it was Jesus' joy, then it's my joy too. God gives freely, without demanding in return. That is the dangerous message of the cross. Nothing you do can or will make a difference in that. God gave for joy. That's all. We give our lives to him for the same joy. Don't turn the Good News into Mostly Good News, Somewhat Good News, or even Bad News. Guilt is not our motivation.

Sacrifice Is Not Blindly Given

Our family was camping in Yosemite with our friends Bryan and Nancy and their kids when someone came running by, shouting that there was a mother bear and her cubs in the meadow. We all ran to see it, stopping at a rope barrier by the path. But two-year-old Jeremy, Bryan and Nancy's son, didn't stop running. He ran under the rope and straight toward the bears.

Everyone yelled, and several of us jumped over the rope in pursuit. But Nancy, with mother speed, outran us all and grabbed Jeremy just feet away from the mother bear, who had turned and put herself between him and her cubs.

Nancy recalled later that even though she was pretty certain she was going to die, she didn't consider doing anything else. She said she had always wondered whether she had it in her to give her life for her children, and now she knew she did. I don't think Nancy was performing a sacrificial act as much as she was living out a sacrificial life. And she did it "with eyes wide open," with complete knowledge of what might happen.

So our sacrifice is done "with eyes wide open to the mercies of God, . . . as an act of intelligent worship" (Romans 12:1 Phillips). We aren't called to close our eyes or minds to the obvious. Sacrifice can be hard; it can feel bad; it can hurt. But we do it anyway, with eyes fixed on the mercies of God.

Sacrifice Is Not a Quid Pro Quo Exchange

God does not count the value of what we offer and return it to us in exact measure. He said of the widow who gave two cents that she had done more than the wealthy who gave much. The servant who invested and earned ten talents was rewarded with the oversight of ten *cities*.

When we keep track of all the sacrifices we've made and the hardships we've endured, are we not hoping to balance the debit and credit columns in our lives to justify ourselves to the God of math? Instead, God invites us to stop counting sins, sacrifices, sorrows, and hardships and to surrender to the One who loves us with an everlasting love.

Sacrifice Is Not Appeasement

It is not the anger of God that compels us to sacrifice, as with Kali, but God's goodness. In view of God's great mercy, Paul calls us to give ourselves to him (Romans 12:1). Our offering of ourselves does not buy favor, but *returns* favor already received.

Interestingly, the Old Testament records God's actually rejecting certain sacrifices, as in the case of Cain's offering of grain instead of an animal. Why are some sacrifices acceptable and some not? Perhaps we should think of it as an artist reaching for the specific brush he needs to paint a line, or a musician finding the instrument that will perfectly express his song; all but the right one are wrong. God knows what he is making of you, and the right sacrifice—the one he reaches for—is the only one that is acceptable and perfect.

NOT ALL ART IS SACRIFICE

I need to say this, or you might get the impression that art comes only through hard work and great discomfort. That is not always the case. Some art is simply a gift. It comes effortlessly. The song "Yesterday" came to Paul McCartney in his sleep. He woke up and began playing it on the piano in his room. (He initially called it "Scrambled Eggs," and the lyrics continued, "Baby, how I love your legs," but good sense prevailed.) Handel's *Messiah* was written in just twenty-one days.

My best-known song, "Lord, Be Glorified," was written in an evening. The simple melody came to me while I was spending time with God in my mother-in-law's living room. I asked God to help me write a song that Cindy and I could sing together before ministering. I had decided not to share it with anyone. I wanted it to be our private prayer. Within moments, the melody came to me and the whole song was written, though it seemed as if I received it in completed form. It was a heavenly gift. It took virtually no work on my part except to transcribe and receive it. I often tell people in concert that in that moment I looked up to heaven and said, "Lord, do you like my song?" And he replied, "No, Bob, do you like *my* song?"

I wish I could say that most songs came that easily. But most come through sacrifice. I have labored over some songs for months and even years, trying to tease out the best idea, trying to fit the lyrics just so. I can assure you, the amount of effort you put into a song does not always equal the amount of "success" that the song has. Some songs are like difficult children—exercises in frustration. They resist shaping, and at the same time they won't go away and leave you alone. They hang around like a painful lesson waiting to be learned.

It's embarrassing to admit, but there have been times when my wife and I wished I could write another "hit" song like "Lord, Be Glorified." It sure would have helped with paying our kids' college bills. But whenever I tried, the act was so sterile and lifeless that it left me empty and depressed. I was trying to use math to get to art. We might as well have tried to come up with an algebraic equation that would produce lovely melodies. It is a great comfort to me that one of my favorite artists, Van Morrison, wrote a song in which he declared that he'd love to write another song to make some money, to pay some bills, and to get some peace of mind.[3]

But then there are those times when melody and

lyric arrive like a package from heaven, already knitted together, already beautiful and simple.

GIVING YOUR MATERIALS TO GOD

Surrendering our lives—our very selves—to God is our way of putting the materials of his art completely at his disposal. We will never be truly who we are without completely abandoning ourselves to Jesus. Only the seed that dies bears fruit, and only the life that is lost will be found.

I recently stood in the wide hall of Florence's Galleria dell'Accademia that leads to the statue of David. In that hall there are four other sculptures by Michelangelo, each an incomplete block or chunk of stone. In one, the face of a figure was nearly finished, and a right arm was visible with a vein crawling across it, sinuous and lifelike. But as I moved around the block of stone, the details of the sculpture became less and less distinct. I could see where Michelangelo had begun to shape a shoulder and the beginning of the drape of a cloak. However, the sculptor's precise chisel marks soon gave way to raw rock—a slab of marble, and nothing more. The whole effect of these four sculptures was eerie and disconcerting, like observing people half born and somehow trapped in the rock and trying to get out. It gave me a sense of regret and loss at what great treasures these might have been had

Michelangelo found the freedom to finish them. Each stone carried so much promise and possibility, yet their incompletion was a kind of rebuke to the whole idea of art.

How many of us are like these sculptures, full of grand possibilities that are never realized because we have not allowed God the freedom to shape us as he wills? It is easy to be stunned by the magnificence of Michelangelo's *David*—seventeen feet of youthful vigor and hope immortalized in stone. Michelangelo was given every opportunity to finish and perfect it. He sought holiness in his art, and he found it. The sculpture is perfect and complete, a purity of vision embodied in marble. This is what God wants for us—to complete his vision in us.

I invite you to stop praying about all the broken things in your life that need fixing. God is not your handyman; he is your Creator. You may replace your prayers for fixing with prayers of surrender because that's where the art begins. Yield to the Master Artist. Let him sacrifice what he will, and you will become a stunning display of art and grace.

8

ART
AND PAIN

A stern discipline pervades all nature,
which is a little cruel that it may be very kind.
Edmund Spenser

Justice will be fully vindicated
when the curtain falls on the present stage,
the house-lights go on,
and we go out into the Real World.
J. B. Phillips

There are a lot of hurting people on airplanes, and I don't mean from turbulence or fear of flying.

I know this because occasionally, and usually against my will, I have conversations with my fellow flyers. One time a Jewish businessman engaged me in conversation and told me he believed that Hitler was a Christian and, therefore, that the Christian God or his people were behind the Holocaust. I told him I didn't think we could find a single Christian who thought Hitler was one of us, but I don't think I changed his mind.

Another time I was flying home from Los Angeles on an almost-empty airplane. For some crazy reason, a woman who was already seated got up and moved into my row. She could have had the entire back of the plane to herself. I thought this was either a character-building annoyance or an appointment from God. I was right.

She wanted to talk about God. She'd had a religious upbringing and had left it behind, but she had kept the feelings of guilt. "If there is a God, he's an—" she said, using a term I won't repeat here.

She then asked the litany of why-is-there-pain-and-suffering-in-the-world questions. I suggested that if God were truly bad, he could surely come up with better ways to torture his little creations than famines, pestilence, and natural disasters.

Then I told her my ideas about math and art. I asked if she could ever see herself as God's art project—if she could imagine that instead of trying to solve her, God wanted to prepare her for his eternal art show. She became silent. Finally she said, "I just don't know that I can see myself that way." I suggested that was how God saw her, even if she couldn't yet. She had tears in her eyes when we exited the plane, and I never saw her again.

Math wants to rid the world of pain. Math is angry at God because there is any pain at all. Math demands that things add up. Math demands a conclusion, verdict, judgment, or solution. Math even boycotts God until the equation makes sense.

But art approaches the "problem" of pain in a way math never can. Art realizes that pain is largely a mystery and that there is no earthly "solution" to it. Art knows that demanding a solution is the wrong way to view our condition. Try as we might, we will never find a solution because pain is not math. It will never add up.

But if pain is art, we can understand immediately because we know how seemingly cruel, brusque, and uncaring an artist can be with his own art, scraping off whole layers of paint, discarding whole chapters of books or reels of film, rewriting the same song over and over in search of artistic perfection. Sometimes an artist will even cause himself hurt in this pursuit.

If God is our Artist and we are his art, would we expect anything less?

ART AND DESTRUCTION

Pain and destruction are part of the artistic process. From the examples of human artists, we know that sometimes they actually become violent with their artwork. Michelangelo, for example, was never satisfied with his art. He belittled it, frequently abandoned it, and destroyed some pieces. Though he made detailed sketches of his sculptures and frescoes before actually working on them, he destroyed all those sketches before he died so that his works, in his words, would "give no other appearance than that of perfection."[1] He even badly damaged the sculpture he was making for his own tomb because he was dissatisfied with how it was turning out.[2]

The Last Judgment section of the Sistine Chapel, an elaborate multitiered fresco measuring forty-eight by forty-four feet, required the destruction of frescoes by a previous artist, a now-obscure man named Perugino. Michelangelo scraped off one of his own sections, called Deluge, from the Sistine Chapel because it would not dry. When the Sistine Chapel frescoes were done, even though they had been rushed to completion by the pope, the pope was so awestruck that he fell to his knees in prayer. Yet Michelangelo still believed, in his own words, that painting "still just isn't my profession."[3]

Some of the most famous writers of the twentieth century wanted their work destroyed and never published. Austrian author Franz Kafka published little and was virtually unknown before his death at a young age. He left notes addressed to his friend and literary executor Max Brod. They read: "Dearest Max, my last request: Everything I leave behind me ... in the way of diaries, manuscripts, letters (my own and others'), sketches, and so on, [is] to be burned unread." Of his already-published books Kafka wrote, "I do not mean that I wish them to be reprinted and handed down to posterity. On the contrary, should they disappear altogether that would please me best.... Everything else of mine ...—all these things without exception are to be burned, and I beg you to do this as soon as possible."[4]

If Brod had followed this instruction, we wouldn't have Kafka's most famous works, such as *The Trial*, which helped to shape the century's literary ethic.

Vladimir Nabokov also demanded that his last novel, written on note cards and kept in an anonymous safe deposit box in Switzerland, be destroyed because he had not been able to perfect it before falling ill. His wife could not bring herself to carry out this wish, so she passed the responsibility on to her son. He read the work and described it as "Father's most brilliant novel, the most concentrated distillation of his creativity."[5] After decades of wrestling with what to do, he decided recently to publish the book.

Even Virgil, the great Roman poet, is said to have instructed his executor to destroy the *Aeneid* because Virgil had not finished editing it. This request was ignored, by order of Caesar. Imagine Western literature without this epic poem.

Why did these artists want their works destroyed? Perhaps they appreciated the idea that destruction is sometimes part of the creative process too, and they wanted to control that aspect of their work as well. Perhaps they felt that their works would embarrass them. I know how they feel. Many times I have listened to my early recordings and cringed. I hope history will not judge me by the synthesized music I made in the 1980s!

I think God sometimes feels this artistic impulse as well. It seems to me, as I read the Bible, that God is at times like a frustrated artist whose creation is abandoning him. He is like a painter who destroys a canvas in utter exasperation. Think of God's mood just before the flood. He was prepared to wipe out the entire human race, so distressed was he. The materials of his art had become so corrupted, so fragmented and unholy, that they were nearly useless. But Noah and his family remained good art. It's almost like God took one last glance at his workshop before turning out the lights and spied a few usable materials in the corner. Instead of closing the door on humanity, God spared them and used Noah's family to remake the canvas.

Or think of Lot's experience in Sodom and Gomorrah, living amid the foul corruption of those two cities. God bemoaned the corruption of his artwork there. Think for a moment about what might have been possible. These two cities could have stood out as places of righteousness. Instead, they were a stench in God's nostrils, like a gourmet recipe somehow spoiled beyond recognition. But before destroying Sodom, God looked for good materials —just a few righteous people. He couldn't find enough. Abraham tried to prevail on him, but God had made his artistic judgment. Like any good artist, God salvaged what was worth saving—Lot's family—and burned the rest.

We see this also in the stories of the prophets and the historical accounts of the Old Testament. God was at turns exultant about the artistic vision he had for Israel and exasperated and despairing about the artwork's present condition. Temperamentally, God reminds me of an artist in the throes of the creative process.

It's a mystery to me, but God seems to come to moments of painful decision, of reenvisioning the work:

"Behold, I will do a new thing," he said (Isaiah 43:19). OK, but why not do the old thing? Something must have happened in the artistic process to make him want to start over.

Am I saying that God destroys or discards us personally? No. As with Noah and Lot and the nation of Israel, God goes to great lengths to preserve his artwork. His mercy extends even to people who have never contemplated surrendering to him. But in working out situations in our lives or in humanity as a whole, the pain and disruption we go through can be great enough to feel like destruction. There is a corollary here to Paul's statement in 1 Corinthians that we will be saved "as one escaping through the flames" (3:15 NIV). In fact, Paul says in verse 13 that the fire will show our work for what it truly is. God will reveal and remove from us all that detracts from the perfection of his art. This is sacrifice, but sometimes it is accompanied by great pain.

In *Gaudy Night*, a mystery novel by Dorothy Sayers, the lead character, Lord Peter Wimsey, tells the novelist Harriet Vane that if she ever dealt honestly with the character in her book in progress, it would make for highly interesting reading. Harriet replies that to do so would hurt too much. Wimsey says, "What would that matter, if it made a good book?"

Wimsey's attitude seems so glib, so offhandedly cruel. Yet in this passage Sayers is giving us a clue to her theology: God is an artist who is more concerned with the final outcome of his art than the pain that may be suffered in the creation of it. In fact, she got this from the apostle Paul, who says in Romans 8:18 that "the sufferings of this present time are not worthy to be compared with the glory which shall be revealed in us."

Hebrews 12:2 also refers to this attitude when it says that Jesus "for the joy that was set before Him endured the cross, despising the shame." What was to be gained was far better than what it cost in shame and pain. The chapter goes on to say that God chastens all those that he loves, and he does so for their benefit, that they might be "partakers of His holiness" (verse 10). Again, we run headlong into holiness, which is God's artistic vision for each one of us.

Perhaps the question "What does it mean?" or "Why is there suffering?" should be replaced by a better one: "Jesus, what can you make of this pain in my life?"

A BAD LIFE?

People tell my sister-in-law, Shelly, that she has had a bad life. You might be tempted to agree, once you hear her story. She and her twin sister were born to a beautiful, jet-setting woman named Jo, who was married to a pilot. But Jo was having an affair with a popular radio show host, Don. One evening Don came by after his radio show to find Jo in an alcoholic stupor, and the girls bruised and crying. He kidnapped the girls and took them on a round-about journey that ended in Puerto Rico.

Jo came after them. She and Don reconciled and decided to rob a bank to get some cash. But then Jo and her new lover, Don's business partner, secretly decided to betray him to the police. When Don ran out of the bank with a bag of money, Jo and the getaway car had vanished. He spent five years in a Puerto Rican jail.

If you're expecting the film credits to roll at this point, rest assured, this really happened.

Jo fled with the girls to Vancouver, Canada. The Canadian authorities didn't want them and put them on a train to anywhere they wanted to go. Jo chose Redding, California, because it was close to Don's relatives.

Jo's drunkenness continued, and she was now steeped in poverty. The girls worked in the school lunchroom just to have something to eat. The kind folks at the market looked the other way when they stole food. Shelly got especially harsh beatings because, as Jo told her, "You look just like your dad." Shelly couldn't understand how one twin could look more like him than the other.

As she lay in bed at night, Shelly would look up at a paper cutout of Jesus that she had been given at a Vacation Bible School and had tacked to the underside of the top bunk. She would talk to it as though Jesus were there with her. It gave her great comfort.

One weekend, Jo called her daughters in from playing and told them, "Girls, say good-bye to your mother. I have just taken enough pills and booze to kill myself." Soon she lay down on the couch and went to sleep forever. The girls cried, but Shelly also thought, "I'm finally free." A Christian family took the girls in. Life suddenly got a lot better.

Shelly married Jeff, my brother-in-law, shortly after high school graduation. They worked hard and lived lean as he studied and finally earned a doctorate in psychology. They and their three kids set up house and enjoyed life. They were strongly committed to Christ and to their local church.

One day their nineteen-year-old son Matt complained of pain in his mouth that wouldn't go away. The doctor looked at him and immediately hospitalized him. He was diagnosed with leukemia. It got worse. They transported him by helicopter to Stanford University Hospital.

The chemotherapy left this athletic, handsome young man bald, bloated, and weak. Jeff and Shelly dropped everything to be with him. Ten months of sitting by his bedside in Palo Alto depleted their funds. Matt died two days before Palm Sunday at twenty years of age. He never lost faith that he would be healed.

Meanwhile, Jeff had been ignoring back pains that were growing increasingly intense. He thought they might be the result of weakness brought on by sitting with Matt day after day. Besides that, he didn't want to complain. It seemed petty in light of what Matt had gone through.

But when he began to have difficulty swallowing water, he thought it might be time to see the doctor. On Valentine's Day, Jeff and Shelly's thirty-second wedding anniversary and just a few months after Matt's death, the doctor told him that he had cancer of the esophagus. Jeff asked what his odds of survival were. "Zero," the doctor told him.

Many people prayed for his healing. But the cancer crept into his spine and up to his brain. As a neuropsychologist, he knew what was happening to him and had no power to stop it. He died a few months prior to my writing this.

In a seventeen-month period, Shelly buried her younger son and her husband. Once the house was full of love and laughter; now she lives alone. They even had to put down the family dog because, after Matt's death, it began to bite children. She came to visit us last weekend, and I asked her to tell me her story again. There was so much more to it than I knew.

But Shelly's response to pain is the healthiest I have ever encountered. She told me, "Every time something bad happens to me, I think, 'What can I make of this?' "

What can I make of this?

That sounds a lot different than, "Why, God?"

She also told me that when people tell her she has had a bad life, she is quick to correct them. She says, "I've had a *life*! Whether it's bad or good is determined not by what happens to you but by what you make of it."

It may not surprise you that Shelly is an artist. A brilliant artist. One of the most gifted painters and illustrators I know. Large canvases of her work, both abstract and realistic, adorn her home and many other homes. Wherever she lives, her dwelling comes alive with color and design.

Shelly lives in the realm of art, and I don't just mean paintbrushes and pencils. She has embraced the mystery of our relationship with Christ, which sometimes takes us through places that cannot be quantified by math. She knows that God is at work for good, to create beauty in her life. She allows him to incorporate every experience —good and bad, big and small—into the masterpiece she is becoming. I can't tell you how much I admire her.

In some people's minds, Shelly has every reason to hate God. They say God took her mother, her father, her son, and her husband. Like the woman on the airplane, they ask what kind of God would do such a thing. They turn away from him and turn back to the frustrating equation that can never be adequately solved.

They don't seem to realize that pain and sorrows can become "found art" in God's hands. "They are wanting," as J. B. Phillips wrote, "a world in which good is rewarded and evil is punished—as in a well-run kindergarten."[6]

Math demands an answer. Art offers every circumstance as artistic material to God.

Math wants it to make sense. Art wants it to be good.

Math smolders with anger and bitterness. Art invites God's creativity into even the worst situations.

Which do you do?

9

HOW TO BE
GREAT ART

As far as I am concerned,
a painting speaks for itself.
What is the use of giving explanations,
when all is said and done?
A painter has only one language.
Pablo Picasso

An artist cannot talk about his art
any more than a plant can discuss horticulture.
Jean Cocteau

I found I could say things with color and
shapes that I couldn't say any other way—
things I had no words for.
Georgia O'Keeffe

A group of aspiring songwriters sat in a room with CDs and lyric sheets of their songs in hand. I was there hoping to help. I've written a lot of mediocre songs and thought they could learn by not doing whatever it was I had done. I was waiting to hear the honest cries of their hearts, the unvarnished expressions of who they really were. Instead, the songwriters all seemed to be telling someone else's story, not their own. The lyrics were uninventive and stayed comfortably in the "day, way," "sky, fly" zone, and the melodies were usually another person's idea dressed up as their own.

Sometimes we live our lives like a copied melody. We see what works for others, and we emulate it without any real thought. We follow the rules, pay our tithes, say our prayers, and attend church. We don't "drink or chew or run with girls that do," as the old Pentecostals say. But something is missing. We've got all logs and no fire.

And then we meet those burning souls who, from moment to moment, seem to be blazing with the Father's joyful art. Their entire *being* is different. They aren't wearing someone else's habits. Rather, they live every moment like it's new. They are singing their own original melody, clearly and from the heart.

God never tries to make *pretty good* art. God wants to change the world. He always swings for the fences. *Pretty good* is math; "God saw all that he had made, and it was very good" is art.

God longs to paint our lives with significance and purpose, to make of us great and lasting art that testifies to his glorious love. He is never derivative, borrowing melodies from others. Will we let God sing the song of us? Will we let him create and color and breathe life into the world around us through the materials we are made of?

BE WILLING TO CHANGE

Just because we are God's works of art does not mean we are presently perfect. Remember that we are in the Artist's studio right now. Things are bound to change.

Amateur songwriters often resist advice because, they say, "God gave me the song, and so it cannot be changed." Oh really? I want to tell them, "Great. If God gave you the song, then don't copyright it or profit from it. It's not yours." The times I've done this I've earned some rather bleak stares.

I believe that God usually gives gifts of creativity, not songs, to people. And changing and improving a song, or any work of art, is part of the process. As works of art in God's hands, we should be open to being changed in ways that surprise us.

If you look carefully at the paintings in the Sistine Chapel, you find that Michelangelo's style changed during the time it took him to paint it. His early depictions of people are small and tightly drawn. The later paintings show humans so full figured and rounded as to seem almost planetary.[1]

Michelangelo was willing to change—and improve. We should be willing too.

ACCEPT LIFE'S GOODNESS— AND ABSURDITY

Some Christians constantly try to make sense of everything. They want to put every life event into eternal perspective immediately. They say, "Oh, I see what God is doing." And then they explain God's perspective on what just took place.

Whether they know it or not, these people hate mystery. They hate the unknown. Yet, as we've discussed, mystery is an essential part of our relationship with God. Mystery cannot be explained, equated, or made to add up. We can talk about it, but we always end up "dancing about architecture." Christians who demand meaning and sense in every life event are being math-minded.

I knew a Christian singer who flatly rejected all Christian instrumental music because he failed to see the meaning or usefulness in it. "What does it mean?"

he said. "It's wasted time that could have been used to preach." He saw music as a tool of logic, with no value in it as art, let alone mystery.

Sometimes life doesn't make sense. It is often absurd. That is the nature of art. It is the nature of the Artist.

I use the word *absurd* on purpose. It is not the same as mysterious. If you don't get absurd humor, you might miss this aspect of God's artistry. My family has always been into absurd jokes. Maybe it's because many of us are ministers. My dad's favorite joke was: What's the difference between a duck? Answer: One leg is shorter than it is. Deep, huh?

When I was five or six, I wrote what can only be considered an absurd near-haiku:

> I climbed a tree
> But the tree wasn't there
> So I fell down

Absurdity is incongruence, nonsense, illogic. But it also points us to art and away from math. For example, from a math point of view, giraffes are absurd. Duck-billed platypuses and slugs are absurd. They are not the solution to some problem. They can only make sense as works of art.

One of the most irritating questions you can ask any artist is: "What does it mean?" The best answer is simply silence. Art cannot be explained. It is what it is. I don't recall anyone asking about a giraffe, "Yes, but what does it mean?" It means giraffe. Ask God to explain koala bears, and his answer is likely to be ... koala bears. How do you quantify koala bears? They just *are*. There is no solution or equation or formula that will help us get their "meaning" any better.

One of the most influential pieces of early twentieth-century art was Pablo Picasso's *Guernica*, depicting the destruction of the town of the same name in 1937 during the Spanish civil war. It was commonly regarded as an anti-war statement and has been extensively used in a propagandist way by various causes, including the Vietnam War. However, when asked to explain the meaning of the strong symbols in the painting, Picasso said:

> This bull is a bull and this horse is a horse.... If you give a meaning to certain things in my paintings it may be very true, but it is not my idea to give this meaning. What ideas and conclusions you have got I obtained too, but instinctively, unconsciously. I make the painting for the painting. I paint the objects for what they are.[2]

Life is like that sometimes too. To try to explain loss, sorrow, beauty, or joy is to reduce it to calculation, a measure of worth, logic. There is no explanation. There is an essential mystery to it that transcends discussion. Yet some people are frustrated at the notion of a universe that doesn't make sense. Many Christians find it unacceptable that God desires goodness over sense or leaves us with a question unanswered. Perhaps they have been taught to expect that they can, with enough prayer and Bible study, understand everything God has done, is doing, and will do. These are like the people who constantly approach an artist and demand, "Yes, but what does it mean?"

But anyone who has lain on their back in the middle of a field and watched fireflies mimic the stars in the night sky enjoyed it not because they could explain it; they were just delighted in the goodness of it. While creation is an intricate system that will reveal its glories to the curious, its complexity doesn't need to be fully understood to be fully enjoyed. A butterfly is simply beautiful, whether or not it makes sense.

Certainly it all makes sense to God. He is the one with the artistic vision for it. If God should decline to give an explanation of his art, are we in a position to demand that he provide one?

"O LORD, how great are Your works! Your thoughts are very deep," wrote the psalmist (Psalm 92:5).

" 'For My thoughts are not your thoughts, nor are your ways My ways,' says the LORD. 'For as the heavens are higher than the earth, so are My ways higher than your ways, and My thoughts than your thoughts' " (Isaiah 55:8–9).

"Great is the mystery of godliness," Paul wrote to

Timothy (1 Timothy 3:16). Paul elsewhere affirms God's heavenly artistic prerogative when he tells us, not that "all things work together to make sense," but that "all things work together *for good*" (Romans 8:28, emphasis added).

Cindy and I were riding along in the car once when a favorite Van Morrison song came on. It caught both of us up and carried us away into speechless rapture. After the song had ended, we let the silence hang around us. There seemed to be a holy hush in the car. Neither of us tried to explain what had happened; we just smiled and rode on.

So when some people always seem to know what God is up to in their lives, I can almost hear the desperate scratching of chalk on a blackboard, their adding this, subtracting that, dividing it by this—and aha! "It all makes sense now. I see exactly where God is heading with this."

Right.

It brings to mind a story in Matthew 26 in which a woman with an alabaster container of expensive perfumed oil broke it and washed the feet of Jesus and then dried them with her hair. The disciples were indignant. "'Why this waste?' they asked. 'This perfume could have been sold at a high price and the money given to the poor'" (verses 8–9 NIV). Jesus replied simply, "She has done a beautiful thing to me" (verse 10 NIV). He didn't even get into the equation. He sidestepped it and pointed instead at the beauty of it. Math, in all its practical, sensible wisdom, was brushed aside in favor of a wasteful, extravagant display of Art.

Doesn't this sound like God at the end of each creation day? "It is good." Not, "It makes sense." Big difference!

If life were merely an equation, the woman's pouring of the perfume on Jesus' feet would have been a senseless act. But life is more than sense. Sometimes it is nonsense.

In John 9, as Jesus passed by a blind man, the disciples asked him whether the man's sins or the sins of his parents were responsible for his blindness. Jesus told them that it was neither, but that the works of God would be displayed in him. Their question was rooted in math: there must be a debit in the column somewhere to account for this punishment. Jesus' reply was art: God wants to show off right here, right now, in this man, whether it makes sense to you or not.

When Jesus told Nicodemus he needed to be "born again" (John 3:3), Nicodemus's response was pure math: "Do I need to crawl back into my mother's womb?!" Nicodemus wanted sense, but Jesus gave him nonsense; he wanted horse, but Jesus gave him giraffe.

This is the point where biblical literalists (like me) get tripped up. We read the Bible like a diagram when it is more like a painting. We look for a plan, but we get poetry. Life can seem to us absurd to an almost grotesque degree. For example, a couple of friends my age have died in the last few years. Two of them died on the toilet. Make no mistake, these were good guys. They lived good lives and had good families. They didn't deserve a death that was more like a punch line. At the same time, how can you not laugh? The circumstances of their passing brought a lot of people joy.

Absurdity is one of God's many art forms. When life becomes absurd, the best thing to do is laugh along.

SEASONS OF LIFE

Songwriting has always been my favorite aspect of what I do, but as a young man I did not realize it was seasonal. I was simply exhilarated by my ability to create something beautiful. But when I went into the autumn and winter of my creative cycle for the first time, I thought for sure that I had lost my gift. I got on my knees and prayed, asking God for redemption and favor. I thought maybe I had done something wrong and that the ability to write had been taken from me. Months passed without even a glimmer of an idea for a song. Then suddenly it returned, and I began to write songs again. I was thrilled!

Then it went away again. I thought God was saying I'd been a bad steward of the songs he'd given back to me. But then the season changed, and the ability came back again. It took me several of these cycles to learn that creativity is seasonal. Trying to write a song at the wrong time is like picking fruit before it is ripe. You must let it mature, give it time, and nurture it.

I think God knows we can take only so much changing at a time. In a story Jesus told, the servant did not ask for a day or a week to try to get the unfruitful tree to bear fruit; he asked for another year (Luke 13:8). A year is a long time. He knew it would take that kind of time. God's artistry in us takes time as well. Sometimes the paint needs to dry. Sometimes the lyrics need to sit for a while.

Leonardo da Vinci gave this advice to young artists: "It is well that you should often leave off work and take a little relaxation, because when you come back to it you are a better judge; for sitting too close at work may greatly deceive you."[3]

Life, like art, is seasonal.

NEVER UNDERESTIMATE THE POWER OF YOUR ART

It was after an evening concert that a young woman approached me. She was well dressed, and from the way she carried herself she appeared to be successful and happy. She introduced herself and said, "Your music kept me alive." I smiled because I thought she was deliberately exaggerating in a lighthearted way. Then I saw the tears well up in her eyes. She said, "I am one of eight children. Six of us are dead. They took their own lives. Only one sister and I are left. I have struggled with the very same depression that troubled my siblings. Except that for the past five years I have listened to your music day and night. It encouraged me to go on. You took me into the throne room with your worship songs. You are the only reason I haven't followed my family into the grave." Now we were both crying.

God's art in us is incomplete. We are all works in progress. But God uses works in progress to bless others. You may feel ordinary, but you should never underestimate the power of your art, even before it is fully complete.

Leo and Gertrude Stein bought Picasso's painting *Three Women*, one of the earliest Cubist paintings, and hung it in the most prominent place in their Paris salon. Artists from all over the world saw and were influenced by that painting. It was not Picasso's greatest work, by most people's estimates, but it influenced the direction of all modern art by influencing other artists.[4]

Let God hang you in a prominent place too, so he can influence others through you, even before you are finished.

BE WILLING TO BREAK
THE ROUTINE

Great art is never rote. If you want rote art, watch the guy painting mountain and ocean scenes on the street corner for twenty-five dollars a canvas. His is not so much art as craft—the ability to reproduce the same visual cliché speedily and many times over without adding any significant new ideas.

I was once pacing behind the curtain on a dark, empty stage in Tacoma, Washington. On the other side of the curtain, the auditorium was filling up with people. Alone, pacing and praying, I asked, "Jesus, what do you want for tonight?"

Understand that I have a set of musical routines I can do almost in my sleep. I sing a funny song about putting God in denominational boxes and follow it with a comedic riff. I talk about my family and what I do, and then I sing a bit called "What if Sinatra, Elvis, the Beatles, or Willie Nelson had written 'Lord, Be Glorified?'" I tell a story about my dad and sing a song I wrote after his death that is stirring and uplifting. I know how to pace a concert to make it an enjoyable time together.

But a set of routines can become a deep rut. As I paced and prayed on that stage in Tacoma, I was asking Jesus to call the shots. I have prayed this prayer many times before, and its intention has been fluid. I have been glib and asked it merely to appear to myself to be sincere and spiritual. I have at times meant this: "Given the set of songs and comments I have already chosen to do, what else would you want, Lord?" I have asked for a positive, dynamic spiritual result that would make me look good and bolster "my" ministry. But as I walked and talked with Jesus that night, I meant it. What did he want for tonight?

His response caught me off guard: "Bring them to me."

That was all. "Bring them to me." I was being offered the inestimable privilege of creating a moment and atmosphere in which God and man could meet. More precisely, I was given permission to come boldly to the God of the universe and bring this audience of people along! If I would bring them to Jesus, he would do what he wanted in them. I understood clearly that I was not to bring them to a good Christian philosophy. I was not required to persuade them of anything. All I was asked to do was to bring them to Jesus.

"Bring them to me." With those four words, my whole plan fell apart. I knew I couldn't step out on the stage and do my song routines. I didn't have an inkling even about where I would start. I felt like Abraham beginning a journey without knowing where he was being led. I was about to go where no Bob Kilpatrick had gone before.

I took my guitar in hand and walked out from behind the curtain into a daring adventure that required me to listen carefully for the still small voice that would, I hoped, guide me through the evening. My hope was realized. I sang the song that came to my mind and then sang the next song that came to my mind. The people responded in worship, and the place was filled with joyful reverence. Suddenly someone was beside me on the stage calling for people who had specific needs to come to the front for prayer. I kept singing as people streamed forward. We spent a long time simply singing our praises as these needs were lifted up to the Lover of our souls.

I don't know all that happened that night, but I do know that we came to Jesus—and Jesus met us there. The last song came to a soft ending. We paused for a few moments in the sweet silence, and then I walked behind the curtain. My heart was at rest. Every time I prepare to stand before an audience now, I think of the simple command: *Bring them to me.*

Has your art become rote? If so, open yourself afresh to the Artist. You may get a surprising new direction.

WORK HARD
TO THE END

Michelangelo's final work, begun when he was in his seventies, was St. Peter's Basilica. He worked on it "solely for the love of God," he said. No longer was rivalry or wealth or reputation a concern. His rivals had all died. His reputation was established. He wouldn't need money much longer. He was coming as close as he ever did to holiness in his art. He died before the Basilica was completed. On his deathbed, he said, "I regret … that I am dying just as I am beginning to learn the alphabet of my profession."[5]

We should all feel the same way—that we never run out of things to do and that we would happily work for another thousand years if God were to give us that time.

ART AND REDEMPTION

My dad was one of God's greatest works of art. God salvaged and redeemed what easily could have been a wrecked life and used the materials to touch unknown thousands of people with God's love.

Augie Kilpatrick spent his youth in the stately, austere Orphan House in Charleston, South Carolina. His father had died of a burst appendix during a hurricane, which kept him from getting medical care. My grandmother had a hard time caring for her six children, so she put some of them in the Orphan House. For reasons she never made clear, she took out all her other children on the same day but left my father in for three additional years, until he was fifteen, at which time he got out as a result of his own effort.

You can imagine what an orphan's life is like—or maybe you can't. Picture waking up as the matrons pile freshly laundered clothes on the floor in the boys' dorm. You suddenly realize you have to scramble and fight for

215

clothes that fit you. Whatever you get are your clothes for the week, no matter how outsized, torn, or stained.

Imagine spitting on your food the moment the plate is set before you so that none of the bigger boys will steal it.

Imagine being the "ball" in a game where the older kids whack the younger ones with a broom.

Now imagine lining up week after week as prospective adoptive parents walk through, looking for a child to take home. Imagine trying to stand as tall as you can—your face clean, your shirt tucked in—hoping that some couple will single you out and say, "Augie, I choose you." Instead, week after week, you watch the adoptive parents say to other children, "Jimmy, I choose you." "Ricky, we choose you." Any kid would start to think there was something wrong with him.

For seven years my dad stood in that line and went through that ritual, and not once did someone say to him, "Augie, I choose you." The matrons had not told him that, even though his mother cared to see him only once a month, she didn't want him to be adopted. He wasn't in the running at all, and yet he was made to stand there, perhaps for show. He would never be chosen, and by the time he found out why, the damage to his soul had been done.

Embittered, he left the orphan house and got a job at the naval shipyard. His approach to life became, "Fine.

If nobody chooses me, then I'm choosing me—so you'd better look out."

He became a fighter. He fought in the rings and in the streets. He cut people with beer bottles in bar fights. He even knocked his own boss out cold. He was determined that no one would ever get the better of him again. He was tough on the outside, but there was still a little orphan boy inside waiting to be chosen.

Then God got hold of my dad. Dad put away riotous living and went to seminary. He felt called to spend his life ministering to those who, like him, had no other place to call home but the house of God. I remember falling asleep on the front pew as he preached in the churches he'd planted in rural Georgia. I remember having potlucks after church under the shade of pine trees, eating fried chicken, black-eyed peas, and watermelon and drinking sweet tea.

But his marriage to my mom began to unravel. He still felt unloved, no matter what she did. The orphan had never left him. One Christmas morning, in the midst of their relational meltdown, he got up early to read the Bible, seeking some consolation. He knelt and laid the Bible on the blue velvet recliner in the living room. Then, without warning, everything around him changed.

The chair and the Bible faded away. He no longer saw his living room but began to have a vision—something

Baptists like him never did. It didn't fit into his theology. But it happened.

He saw his five-year-old self standing straight and smart in tattered clothes on a Saturday in the Charleston Orphan House. The little boy was waiting and hoping to be chosen. As he watched his younger self, all the sensations of that painful time rushed back with horrible strength.

Then a figure approached. It was a father, but not just any father—it was Father God. The Father reached down and picked the little boy up in his arms, hugged him, and held him close. "Augie, I choose you," the Father said.

That moment became the hinge point in my dad's life. He was never the same. He became whole on the inside. My parents experienced a renewal in their marriage and went on to have a worldwide marriage ministry.

He died unexpectedly on July 13, 1991. I suppose you could say that Jesus "solved my dad's problem" by giving him that vision, but I think of it differently. God made a mystical movie, replaying a short reel of footage from a painful past, and then injected something new into the story—himself! The presence of Jesus in those memories redeemed the damaged artwork of my dad's life. My dad went on to become a masterpiece. His life was like a good symphony, going from allegro to agitato, then bellicoso, cambiare, con brio, crescendo, dolcissimo, diminuendo, and ending a niente—a soft, graceful conclusion to a love-saturated life.

There is a great promise for you and me in this story. God does not have favorites. He is not partial to any one of us (Romans 2:11). He doesn't love my dad any more than he loves you and me. God wants to hold you close, call you by name, and say to you, "I choose you."

He chooses you so he can display a work of art that has never been seen before.

He chooses you to become a masterpiece that surpasses anything human hands have ever formed.

He chooses you to be his poem, his painting, his play, his song.

He chooses you to be part of an eternal art show.

Sometimes in concert, when I finish a song, I back away from the microphone. As the audience claps, I know that I am surrounded by others too—the great cloud of witnesses the author of Hebrews describes (12:1)—and I see my father, cheering me on.

I know that one day, when God's artwork in me is finished, I will join him—and you will too. Those who have gone before us are eagerly awaiting the art show God is preparing, which the Bible refers to as "the glory that will be revealed" (Romans 8:18 NIV). No eye has seen, no ear has heard what wonders we actually will become when God is finished with us. Even now, I can almost hear heaven cheering us on as God completes his work in us.

One day the lights will go up and the curtain will rise, and we will take our place forever in the incomparable gallery where the Creator of the universe keeps his greatest works. Then we will know that our time on earth was well spent, the sacrifices well worth it, because the Master took the materials of our lives and made us into masterpieces.

NOTES

Chapter 2: Art and Anti-Art

1. Søren Kierkegaard, *Purity of Heart Is to Will One Thing* (New York: Harper, 1956), 60.

2. Robert Coughlan, *The World of Michelangelo, 1475–1564* (Alexandria, Va.: Time-Life Books, 1966), 85.

Chapter 3: The Art of Loving Relationships

1. Bruce Cockburn, "Laughter," © 1978 by Golden Mountain Music Corp., from the album *Further Adventures of...* Used by permission.

2. Quoted in Phoebe Pool, *Impressionism* (New York: Thames and Hudson, 1985), 88, 93, 95.

3. W. H. Lewis, ed., *Letters of C. S. Lewis* (London: Geoffrey Bles, 1966), 197.

4. Quoted in David Sweetman, *Van Gogh: His Life and His Art* (New York: Crown, 1990), 256.

5. Pool, *Impressionism*, 54.

6. Quoted in Pepe Karmel, *Picasso and the Invention of Cubism* (New Haven, Conn.: Yale University Press, 2003), 10.

7. Pool, *Impressionism*, 54.

8. Humphrey Carpenter, ed., with the assistance of Christopher Tolkien, *The Letters of J. R. R. Tolkien* (Boston: Houghton Mifflin, 2000), 366.

9. Robert Coughlan, *The World of Michelangelo, 1475–1564* (Alexandria, Va.: Time-Life Books, 1966), 86–87.

10. Benvenuto Cellini, *The Autobiography of Benvenuto Cellini* (New York: Penguin, 1998), 18.

11. Coughlan, *The World of Michelangelo*, 94–95.

12. Irma A. Richter, ed., *Selections from the Notebooks of Leonardo da Vinci* (London: Oxford University Press, 1952), 220–21.

13. Carpenter, ed., *Letters of J. R. R. Tolkien*, 302.

14. Debora Silverman, *Van Gogh and Gauguin: The Search for Sacred Art* (New York: Farrar, Straus and Giroux, 2000), 3.

15. Silverman, *Van Gogh and Gauguin*, 3, 271.

16. Carpenter, ed., *Letters of J. R. R. Tolkien*, 349.

17. Pool, *Impressionism*, 167.

18. Coughlan, *The World of Michelangelo*, 151.

19. Carpenter, ed, *Letters of J. R. R. Tolkien*, 341.

Chapter 4: The Art of the Spiritual Disciplines

1. Malcolm Gladwell, *Outliers: The Story of Success* (New York: Little, Brown and Co., 2008).

2. Charles Williams, *War in Heaven* (Grand Rapids: Eerdmans, 1930), 51, 137, 240.

Chapter 5: The Art of Sharing Our Faith

1. Saint Irenaeus, *Adversus Haereses*, book 4, chapter 20, paragraph 7.

Chapter 7: The Art of Sacrifice

1. Irma A. Richter, ed., *Selections from the Notebooks of Leonardo da Vinci* (London: Oxford University Press, 1952), 282.

2. "Notes on Art Matters," *The New York Times*, December 31, 1900.

3. Van Morrison, "I'd Love to Write Another Song," © 1989 by Polydor Records (label of Universal Music Group), from the album *Avalon Sunset*.

Chapter 8: Art and Pain

1. Robert Coughlan, *The World of Michelangelo, 1475–1564* (Alexandria, Va.: Time-Life Books, 1966), 92, 96.

2. See Jack Wasserman et al., *Michelangelo's Florence* Pietà (Princeton, N.J.: Princeton University Press, 2003).

3. Coughlan, *The World of Michelangelo*, 125.

4. Quoted in Kathi Diamant, *Kafka's Last Love* (New York: Basic Books, 2003), 131–32.

5. Quoted in Peter Quennell, *Vladimir Nabokov, His Life, His Work, His World* (New York: Morrow, 1980), 129.

6. J. B. Phillips, *Your God Is Too Small* (New York: Macmillan, 1961), 50.

Chapter 9: How to Be Great Art

1. See Robert Coughlan, *The World of Michelangelo, 1475–1564* (Alexandria, Va.: Time-Life Books, 1966), 125, 128.

2. "Guernica: Testimony of War," *Treasures of the World* series. *PBS.org. www.pbs.org/treasuresoftheworld/guernica /gmain.html.* (Accessed July 29, 2010.)

3. Irma A. Richter, ed., *Selections from the Notebooks of Leonardo da Vinci* (London: Oxford University Press, 1952), 220–21.

4. Cited in Pepe Karmel, *Picasso and the Invention of Cubism* (New Haven, Conn.: Yale University Press, 2003), 29.

5. Quoted in Coughlan, *The World of Michelangelo*, 180, 192.